New Directions for Child and Adolescent Development

Reed W. Larson
Lene Arnett Jensen
EDITORS-IN-CHIEF

William Damon
FOUNDING EDITOR

Social Network Analysis and Children's Peer Relationships

Philip C. Rodkin
Laura D. Hanish
EDITORS

Number 118 • Winter 2007
Jossey-Bass
San Francisco

SOCIAL NETWORK ANALYSIS AND CHILDREN'S PEER RELATIONSHIPS
Philip C. Rodkin, Laura D. Hanish (eds.)
New Directions for Child and Adolescent Development, no. 118
Reed W. Larson, Lene Arnett Jensen, Editors-in-Chief

© 2007 Wiley Periodicals, Inc., A Wiley Company. All rights reserved.

No part of this publication may be reproduced, stored in a retrieval system, or transmitted in any form or by any means, electronic, mechanical, photocopying, recording, scanning, or otherwise, except as permitted under Sections 107 or 108 of the 1976 United States Copyright Act, without either the prior written permission of the Publisher or authorization through payment of the appropriate per-copy fee to the Copyright Clearance Center, 222 Rosewood Drive, Danvers, MA 01923; (978) 750-8400, fax (978) 646-8600. Requests to the Publisher for permission should be addressed to the Permissions Department, John Wiley & Sons, Inc., 111 River St., Hoboken, NJ 07030, (201) 748-6011, fax (201) 748-6008, www.wiley.com/go/permissions.

Microfilm copies of issues and articles are available in 16mm and 35mm, as well as microfiche in 105mm, through University Microfilms, Inc., 300 North Zeeb Road, Ann Arbor, Michigan 48106-1346.

ISBN: 978-0-470-25966-5

NEW DIRECTIONS FOR CHILD AND ADOLESCENT DEVELOPMENT is part of The Jossey-Bass Education Series and is published quarterly by Wiley Subscription Services, Inc., a Wiley company, at Jossey-Bass, 989 Market Street, San Francisco, California 94103-1741. Periodicals postage paid at San Francisco, California, and at additional mailing offices. Postmaster: Send address changes to New Directions for Child and Adolescent Development, Jossey-Bass, 989 Market Street, San Francisco, CA 94103-1741.

New Directions for Child and Adolescent Development is indexed in Cambridge Scientific Abstracts (CSA/CIG), CHID: Combined Health Information Database (NIH), Contents Pages in Education (T&F), Current Abstracts (EBSCO), Educational Research Abstracts Online (T&F), ERIC Database (Education Resources Information Center), Index Medicus/MEDLINE/PubMed (NLM), Linguistics & Language Behavior Abstracts (CSA/CIG), Psychological Abstracts/PsycINFO (APA), Social Services Abstracts (CSA/CIG), SocINDEX (EBSCO), and Sociological Abstracts (CSA/CIG).

SUBSCRIPTION rates: For the U.S., $85 for individuals and $258 for institutions. Please see ordering information page at end of journal.

EDITORIAL CORRESPONDENCE should be e-mailed to the editors-in-chief: Reed W. Larson (larsonr@uiuc.edu) and Lene Arnett Jensen (ljensen@clarku.edu).

Jossey-Bass Web address: www.josseybass.com

Contents

1. Bridging Children's Social Development and Social Network 1
Analysis
Laura D. Hanish, Philip C. Rodkin
The introduction places contemporary social network science within a historical context and highlights the conceptual and methodological advances that underlie each chapter in this volume.

2. Using the Q-Connectivity Method to Study Frequency of 9
Interaction with Multiple Peer Triads: Do Preschoolers' Peer
Group Interactions at School Relate to Academic Skills?
Laura D. Hanish, Hélène Barcelo, Carol Lynn Martin, Richard A. Fabes, Jennifer Holmwall, Francisco Palermo
The Q-connectivity method differentiates peer groups that are enduring versus transient, making clear the development of preschool social networks and their relevance to school success.

3. Social Integration Between African American and European 25
American Children in Majority Black, Majority White, and
Multicultural Elementary Classrooms
Philip C. Rodkin, Travis Wilson, Hai-Jeong Ahn
Does being the racial majority, in society or in the classroom, influence patterns of social integration and animosity between black and white elementary school students?

4. Features of Groups and Status Hierarchies in Girls' and Boys' 43
Early Adolescent Peer Networks
Scott D. Gest, Alice J. Davidson, Kelly L. Rulison, James Moody, Janet A. Welsh
Are boys' and girls' groups really so different? Prevailing theories of gender segregation are put to the test as the authors analyze relative density, status differentiation, and distinctiveness in peer social networks in grades 5 through 7.

5. Statistical Analysis of Friendship Patterns and Bullying 61
Behaviors Among Youth
Dorothy L. Espelage, Harold D. Green Jr., Stanley Wasserman
Using exponential random graph modeling, also known as p^*, the authors show how aggression operates through the social networks of seventh-grade students.

6. Early Adolescent Antisocial Behavior and Peer Rejection: 77
A Dynamic Test of a Developmental Process
John M. Light, Thomas J. Dishion
SIENA, a social network methodology specifically designed for interdependent, developmental data, is used to test whether confluence leads to deviant peer groups across eight middle schools.

7. New Perspectives on Social Networks in the Study of Peer 91
Relations
Antonius H. N. Cillessen
Using a social networks lens, this first commentator suggests that the traditional division of individuals, dyads, and groups may not suffice for modeling the complex structure of children's peer relations.

8. Studying the Individual Within the Peer Context: Are We on 101
Target?
Thomas W. Farmer
The second commentator recalls lessons learned from Urie Bronfrenbrenner and Robert Cairns, including the importance of interpersonal synchrony, complementarity, and social context.

Index 109

How do we study peer relationships and the socialization processes that occur within them? Social network analysis provides tools that can be used to answer questions about the structure and organization of peer relationships and the ways in which children influence one another.

Bridging Children's Social Development and Social Network Analysis

Laura D. Hanish, Philip C. Rodkin

There is no doubt that the growing interdisciplinary field of network science involving nodes and the links that connect them has wide appeal and broad relevance. In a 2006 *New York Times Magazine* article, Patrick Radden Keefe observed that "during the last decade, mathematicians, physicists, and sociologists have advanced the scientific study of networks, identifying surprising commonalities among the ways airlines route their flights, people interact at cocktail parties, and crickets synchronize their chirps." Network science offers sophisticated analytical tools for determining how units (such as elements, airlines, or centers of influence) interact with one another and organize the systems in which they function. The human side of network science, social network analysis, offers a new look at classic questions of individuals within society that psychologists and sociologists have studied for over a century. In a network analysis, social structure and social influence are measured and mapped, making what is powerful, but so often hidden from view, observable to the scientist. But nowhere in the *Times Magazine* story is there mention of children, adolescents, or dynamic, temporal analysis. Of all the

---

This research was supported by grants to L.D.H. from the National Institute of Child Health and Human Development (R01 HD45816) and the National Science Foundation (0338864) and to P.C.R. from the National Institute of Child Health and Human Development (R03 HD48491-01) and the Spencer Foundation (Small Grant 20050079).

professions investing in network analysis—engineering, business, international relations, and more—applications to child and adolescent development lag far behind, yet social network and social development concerns were once joined in a common enterprise, and so they could be again.

The origins of network science lie in no small part with the eccentric therapist Jacob Moreno (and his brilliant but underrecognized collaborator, Helen Jennings; see Freeman, 2004; Jennings, 1943). Moreno's signature 1934 volume, *Who Shall Survive?*, featured careful studies of children from kindergarten to high school and examined childhood phenomena as varied as gender segregation, aggression, ethnic and national differences, leadership, and peer rejection. Linkages between social development and social networks remained strong for a generation after *Who Shall Survive?* was published. Urie Bronfrenbrenner cut his teeth on social network questions such as the correct calculation of high social status (Bronfenbrenner, 1943; Chapter Eight, this volume). Muzafer Sherif (1956) built sociograms to track the evolving network structures of teams of boys who competed and collaborated with one another at Robbers Cave. Bronfrenbrenner's and Sherif's investment in social networks reflected their theoretical commitment to dynamic questions about individuals in society; their scientific commitment to lawful, accurate description and prediction; and their societal commitment to children's health and growth.

Despite these strong, early ties, Moreno's vision of a developmental network science has not yet reached its full potential. In a 1998 *New Directions for Child and Adolescent Development* chapter, "The Popularity of Friendships and the Neglect of Social Networks," Robert Cairns, Hongling Xie, and Man-Chi Leung explained how child development scholarship had dropped out of the social network research scene. They outlined many of the challenges that have resulted in a neglect of social networks among child development researchers. From a theoretical standpoint, individually oriented psychologists suspected that network-level constructs were epiphenomenal once dyadic relationships were taken into account (but see Chapter Five, this volume), and the dominant sociometric techniques of the 1980s and 1990s stressed social status (as measured by likability) and friendships, not the sociograms and group structures of years past (Cillessen & Bukowski, 2000; Renshaw, 1981).

From a methodological standpoint, obtaining quality network data can be difficult. How do we know a group when we see it? Do we trust children's self-reports of the groups to which they belong? Different strategies may be needed when measuring the networks of younger versus older children and in distinct ecologies like school, home, and the community. From a data analysis standpoint, network data are often formidable and frustrating. Multiple-group members break independence assumptions, classifying the presence or absence of relational ties can seem arbitrary, and the quantitative training of child development researchers omits graph-theoretic concepts that are foundational to modern social network analysis. Overlaying these challenges is that the coin of the realm of developmental research—dynamic analysis over multiple time intervals—is hard to reconcile with the static, structural emphasis of traditional network analysis. These barriers have left understanding of children's social networks disconnected from mainstream developmental scholarship and from the expertise of today's social network scientists.

Looking Forward

Social network analysis enables the peer relations researcher to move beyond discrete dyadic relationships such as mutual friendships to relationships that exist among larger groups of peers. Thus, it is possible to determine, for example, how large and dense children's peer networks are, how central children are within their networks, the various structural configurations that characterize social groups, and which peers make up individual children's networks. Social network analysis methods make it feasible to understand the child within his or her social system, enhancing the ability to study socialization processes that draw children toward or away from particular peers as well as those that contribute to peer influence.

Aggression researchers have made particular use of network concepts and methods (Rodkin & Wilson, 2007). For example, the relationship between bullies and victims extends to many of the peers in the elementary classroom. Many children who are not themselves aggressive validate bullies with applause or play supporting roles in bully-led peer groups (Salmivalli, Huttunen, & Lagerspetz, 1997). Social support for aggressive behaviors can amplify children's own and others' aggression over time (Espelage, Holt, & Henkel, 2003). Iatrogenic effects in violence-reduction programs that group high-risk youth, where the intervention proves worse than the control, demonstrate that peer influence can overwhelm adults' best intentions (Dodge, Dishion, & Lansford, 2006). Peer contagion effects can be seen across development, providing evidence that peer socialization processes are at play for young children and adolescents alike (Hanish, Martin, Fabes, Leonard, & Herzog, 2005).

Building on this research, a primary goal of this volume of *New Directions for Child and Adolescent Development* is to demonstrate the wide applicability of social network methods. Group influences are embedded within the totality of children's personality and social development, from gender (Maccoby, 1998), to intergroup relations (Sherif, 1956), to achievement (Kindermann, 1998; Ryan, 2001). Thus, this volume offers important new contributions to the aggression literature (Chapters Five and Six), and other chapters investigate such varied phenomena as the structure of gender-based peer groups(Chapter Four), intergroup relations between African American and European American children (Chapter Three), and early academic achievement (Chapter Two). The value of social network analysis to developmental science includes and generalizes beyond the study of aggression.

Another goal of this volume is to demonstrate methodological advances in social network analysis that have arisen in the past decade, making it possible to move beyond the barriers outlined by Cairns et al. in 1998. Diverse social network methods provide the opportunity to tackle two critical developmental challenges: developmental dynamics and nested contexts. With regard to developmental dynamics, the structuralist perspective of social network analysis is a challenge to researchers who value dynamic, microdevelopmental processes. Contributions to this volume, which benefit from the multidisciplinary expertise of developmentalists, sociologists, statisticians, and mathematicians, infuse dynamic methods into basic concepts of social network analysis, generating potential for sophisticated models where the temporal dimension is given its proper due (see Chapters Two, Four, and Six). With regard to context, the chapter authors recognize the group and go beyond it, connecting the child through his or her networks to multiple social systems. Coleman's *The Adolescent Society* (1961) reported strong differences from school to school in the makeup and values of peer social structures—but where Coleman bemoaned the absence of quantitative techniques for linking the individual to the group, and from there to the school and community, prospects of conceptual and analytical bridges are now apparent (see Chapters Three and Six).

Chapter Overview

The chapters in this volume are organized to demonstrate the applicability of social network methods across the preschool, middle childhood, and early adolescent periods.

Although peer group influence is often thought to be a predominantly postpubescent phenomenon, the reality is that peer groups have the potential to become influential as soon as children are organized into collectivities (Hanish et al., 2005; Martin & Fabes, 2001). Group influence begins in the preschool years, but it is hard to track due to the difficulties of obtaining quality data from young children and the lack of conceptual models guiding how social networks are structured as they emerge in ontogeny. In Chapter Two, Laura Hanish and colleagues introduce readers to the significance of social networks for young children using the Q-connectivity method. This new method is sensitive to such temporal, developmental concepts as how often a child interacts within multiple preschool peer groups, because it considers the day-to-day frequency of children's interactions with one another. Applying the method to understand children's real-world functioning, these authors show that preschool children's sustained interactions with peer groups may be related to their reading and mathematics achievement. They also find that social and academic spheres are connected among preschool children as they are in kindergarten (Ladd, Birch, & Buhs, 1999) and adolescence (Ryan, 2001).

In Chapter Three, Philip Rodkin, Travis Wilson, and Hai-Jeong Ahn tackle the issue of intergroup relations between African American and European American children by examining racial integration and segregation in three distinct classroom contexts: majority black, majority white, and multi-cultural. Drawing on several measures of children's peer relationships—the positive sentiments of mutual friendship, peer group affiliation, and mutual liking, and also the negative sentiment of mutual dislike—the authors show dramatically different patterns of social integration in elementary classrooms that differ in their average ethnic composition. Specifically, in majority black and multicultural classrooms, segregation, whether measured by indexes of positive sentiment or negative sentiment, was low. However, in majority white classrooms, segregation of African Americans was high due to preferences on the part of African American students to affiliate with one another as well as to relatively high rates of rejection of African American students by white students. The authors' findings emphasize the importance of considering how networks function within broader social contexts.

A robust feature of children's peer relationships is that they are strongly gender segregated, such that boys play predominantly with other boys and girls play predominantly with other girls (Maccoby, 1998). This has led Maccoby (1998) and others to coin the two-cultures theory, which posits several differences in the characteristics of girls' and boys' peer groups: boys' groups are hypothesized to be large, cohesive, and centralized, whereas girls' relationships are thought to be more cooperative and dyadic. However, prior research has produced equivocal findings, raising more questions than answers about gender differences in peer social structures. In Chapter Four, Scott Gest and colleagues used a two-year longitudinal design that bridges the transition from middle childhood to early adolescence to study changes in boys' and girls' group structures. Contrary to the two-cultures hypothesis, they found more similarities than differences in boys' and girls' social groups, leading them to conclude that asymmetry in group structures may not be central to explaining the emergence of gender differences.

Chapters Five and Six are notable for their applications of innovative social network methods to unanswered questions about young adolescents' bullying and aggressive behaviors. In Chapter Five, Dorothy Espelage, Harold Green Jr., and Stanley Wasserman apply the new p^* analysis, which is well suited for unpacking the complex structure of peer relationships, to consider how similarities in adolescents' attitudes toward bullying underlie peer group formation. Specifically, p^* is a social network analysis technique that enables developmentalists to define and build peer groups, starting from the simple dyad and moving to triads and larger cliques with various configurations (Robins, Pattison, Kalish, & Lusher, 2007). Essentially p^* permits researchers to recreate the structure of peer relationships across the entire social landscape with very little loss of information, thereby representing in detail how children and adolescents interact and influence one another. Such a complete map of the peer context makes it possible to demonstrate how peer socialization processes, such as homophily (spending time with similar peers), contribute to the formation of peer groups. As

Espelage, Green, and Wasserman show, aggressive homophily is a contagious behavior that organizes adolescents' peer networks.

In Chapter Six, John Light and Thomas Dishion employ SIENA modeling, a groundbreaking social network technique melding tenets of dynamic systems, such as temporally dependent self-organization, with widely used network science indexes such as outdegree, reciprocity, and transitivity. By integrating multiple assessments over time and considering the eight schools in their sample separately, Light and Dishion bring new complexity to the confluence hypothesis, which suggests that deviant peer groups form among aggressive adolescents, who then socialize one another through emergent antisocial norms. Their findings of between-school differences in the peer socialization of antisocial adolescents highlight the fact that different school contexts structure peer interactions in different ways.

Conclusion

Commentaries by Antonius Cillessen in Chapter Seven and Thomas Farmer in Chapter Eight go beyond the particulars of each investigation to address the broader significance of this collection for science and society. Cillessen reflects on the traditional peer relations distinctions of individuals, dyads, and groups. He suggests that we should spend more time seeking to understand how nested individual, dyadic, and group factors work together than on how they can be distinguished. Farmer's commentary elucidates three important goals for the developmental social network science of the future: understanding interpersonal synchrony as a driving psychological force of social networks, linking children's networks to their classroom and school and family ecologies, and accounting for developmental regularity produced by the adults who design educational institutions for children.

This volume of *New Directions for Child and Adolescent Development* is intended to encourage new research and insights into the structure, organization, and function of social networks across the developmental spectrum. We hope to make sense of the innumerable social contacts that children create and are part of, documenting their impact on the here-and-now and in the longer term for the child. Life's confusing realities—boys and girls, a myriad of ethnicities, success in school, aggression, altruism, having and losing status, friends and enemies—are encountered by children who use one another, imperfectly, as a guide. The early view of social network analysis as envisioned by Jennings and Moreno, Bronfenbrenner and Sherif, Coleman and Cairns, was that children and youth create small but growing societies that can be described and mapped. Those maps can be used to understand how children cope with, interpret, and master their enduring and acute challenges: the need to do homework, the desire to learn, the decision to make that bully friend or foe, with whom to interact and become friends. Will quantitative understanding of the permeable boundaries between individual and society, self and other, lead to more complete formulations of social and personality development? Will detailed knowledge of child and adolescent social networks translate into more effective attempts to bolster adjustment and minimize dysfunction? This is the potential of social network analysis when grounded in the life functioning of youth.

References

Bronfenbrenner, U. (1943). A constant frame of reference for sociometric research. *Sociometry, 6,* 363–397.
Cairns, R. B., Xie, H., & Leung, M-C. (1998). The popularity of friendship and the neglect of social networks: Toward a new balance. In W. M. Bukowski & A. H. Cillessen (Eds.), *Sociometry then and now: Building on six decades of measuring children's experiences with the peer group* (pp. 25–53). San Francisco: Jossey-Bass.
Cillessen, A.H.N., & Bukowski, W. M. (2000). Conceptualizing and measuring peer acceptance and rejection. In A.H.N. Cillessen & W. M. Bukowski (Eds.), *Recent advances in the measurement of acceptance and rejection in the peer system* (pp. 3–10). San Francisco: Jossey-Bass.
Coleman, J. S. (1961). *The adolescent society: The social life of the teenager and its impact on education.* New York: Free Press.
Dodge, K. A., Dishion, T. J., & Lansford, J. E. (2006). Deviant peer influences in intervention and public policy for youth. *Social Policy Report, 1,* 1–20.
Espelage, D. L., Holt, M., & Henkel, R. (2003). Examination of peer-group contextual effects on aggression during early adolescence. *Child Development, 74,* 205–220.
Freeman, L. C. (2004). *The development of social network analysis: A study in the sociology of science.* Vancouver, BC: Booksurge.
Hanish, L. D., Martin, C. L., Fabes, R. A., Leonard, S., & Herzog, M. (2005). Exposure to externalizing peers in early childhood: Homophily and peer contagion processes. *Journal of Abnormal Child Psychology, 33,* 267–281.
Jennings, H. (1943). *Leadership and isolation: A study of personality in inter-personal relations.* White Plains, NY: Longmans, Green.
Keefe, P. R. (2006, March 12). Can network theory thwart terrorists? *New York Times.* Retrieved March 12, 2006, from http://www.nytimes.com.
Kindermann, T. (1998). Children's development within peer groups: Using composite social maps to identify peer networks and to study their influences. In W. M. Bukowski & A. H. Cillessen (Eds.), *Sociometry then and now: Building on six decades of measuring children's experiences with the peer group* (pp. 55–82). San Francisco: Jossey-Bass.
Ladd, G. W., Birch, S. H., & Buhs, E. S. (1999). Children's social and scholastic lives in kindergarten: Related spheres of influence? *Child Development, 70,* 1373–1400.
Maccoby, E. E. (1998). *The two sexes: Growing up apart, coming together.* Cambridge, MA: Harvard University Press.
Martin, C. L., & Fabes, R. A. (2001). Testability and consequences of young children's same-sex peer interactions. *Developmental Psychology, 37,* 431–446.
Moreno, J. L. (1934). *Who shall survive? A new approach to the problem of human interrelations.* Washington, DC: Nervous and Mental Disease Publishing.
Renshaw, P. D. (1981). The roots of peer interaction research: A historical analysis of the 1930s. In S. R. Asher & J. M. Gottman (Eds.), *The development of children's friendships* (pp. 1–25). Cambridge: Cambridge University Press.
Robins, G., Pattison, P., Kalish, Y., & Lusher, D. (2007). An introduction to exponential random graph (p*) models for social networks. *Social Networks, 29,* 173–191.

Rodkin, P. C., & Wilson, T. (2007). Aggression and adaptation: Psychological record, educational promise. In P. Hawley, T. D. Little, & P. C. Rodkin (Eds.), *Aggression and adaptation: The bright side to bad behavior* (pp. 233–265). Mahwah, NJ: Erlbaum.

Ryan, A. (2001). The peer group as a context for the development of young adolescent motivation and achievement. *Child Development, 72,* 1135–1150.

Salmivalli, C., Huttunen, A., & Lagerspetz, K.M.J. (1997). Peer networks and bullying in schools. *Scandinavian Journal of Psychology, 38,* 305–312.

Sherif, M. (1956). Experiments in group conflict. *Scientific American, 195,* 54–58.

LAURA D. HANISH is an associate professor of child development in the School of Social and Family Dynamics, Program in Family and Human Development at Arizona State University in Tempe, Arizona.

PHILIP C. RODKIN is an associate professor of child development in the Departments of Educational Psychology and Psychology at the University of Illinois at Urbana-Champaign.

A new social network method shows that young children vary in their abilities to interact with multiple peer groups and to maintain group interactions over time. Learning how to competently sustain group interactions is an important developmental task for preschoolers and is associated with enhanced school readiness, particularly for girls.

Using the Q-Connectivity Method to Study Frequency of Interaction with Multiple Peer Triads: Do Preschoolers' Peer Group Interactions at School Relate to Academic Skills?

Laura D. Hanish, Hélène Barcelo, Carol Lynn Martin, Richard A. Fabes, Jennifer Holmwall, Francisco Palermo

How, when, and under what conditions do peer interactions contribute to variations in developmental trajectories along dimensions that are important to children's well-being? These compelling and fundamental questions have piqued the interest of developmental scientists and led to studies of the ways in which peers socialize and affect such significant developmental outcomes as academic motivation and achievement (Kindermann, 1993). However, scientific advances in this area have been hampered by methodological challenges that make it difficult to quantify children's peer relationships above and beyond specific dyadic or group relationships such as best

---

This research was supported in part by grants from the National Institute of Child Health and Human Development awarded to L.D.H, C.L.M., and R.A.F. (1 R01 HD45816); from the National Security Agency (H98230-05-1-0256) awarded to H.B.; and from the National Science Foundation awarded to William Griffin, L.D.H, H.B., C.L.M., and R.A.F (0338864). Research support for this project was also provided by the Cowden Endowment Fund. We thank the students who contributed to this project and the children, families, and teachers for their participation. Special thanks go to Mike Dodd for software development.

friendships or membership in cliques. We tackle this problem here by introducing a new method, the Q-connectivity method (Barcelo & Laubenbacher, 2005), that provides unique information about children's social structures and then demonstrating one way in which this method can be used to explore whether and under what circumstances preschoolers' interactions with groups of peers (an important aspect of young children's social relations because it is a developmentally sophisticated form of play) contribute to early academic readiness.

Methodological Challenges to Studying Peer Relations

Knowledge of the peers with whom children spend their time is essential to understanding the potential for peer socialization. This knowledge can be difficult to acquire, however, because peer interactions and relationships are complex and can involve various dyadic and group configurations (see Chapter Five, this volume). To illustrate, one child may engage in mutually defined friendships with three different peers, be a member of a peer group that includes those three peers plus two others, and play occasionally with four other peers. A second child may play almost exclusively with two children, exhibiting a pattern of social relationships that is distinctive from the first child. Moreover, because peer relationships are dynamic and change in structure and organization over time, children may form new relationships with peers or dissolve old ones. In addition, the quality and nature of interactions can vary considerably from child to child, relationship to relationship, and time to time; variations that reflect the degree of cooperation versus antagonism, for example, may have considerable, and differential, influence on children.

For all of these reasons, it is difficult to adequately represent children's social landscapes in ways that can be readily analyzed and understood. Methods for studying peers, such as friendship or sociometric nominations, which focus on the individual as a unit of analysis, are an ideal choice for studying individual-level relationship features such as social status, as well as for studying some well-defined aspects of dyadic relationships, such as number of friends. However, these methods are less adaptable for answering questions about children's involvement with peers that extend beyond specific dyadic relationships to, say, mutual friendships. To do this, researchers have often relied on social network methods, which can be used to differentiate the peer groups, usually consisting of a few to several children, that exist within larger units (such as classrooms, grade levels, or schools) and to identify the children who are members of groups (and the group to which they belong) and the children who are isolated (Cairns, Cairns, Neckerman, Gest, & Gariepy, 1988; Richards & Rice, 1981). Social network methods make it possible, even desirable, to use groups as the level of analysis. However, many commonly used statistical techniques are designed for analyzing individual cases rather than grouped data, and specialized analytical tools are needed to use the group as the level of analysis.

Furthermore, by making groups the unit of analysis, sample size requirements are greatly increased over and above what would be needed for individual-level analyses.

Clearly additional methods are needed that can increase the range and flexibility of options for studying peers, peer relationships, and the socialization processes that occur within them. In this chapter, we present the Q-connectivity method (Barcelo & Laubenbacher, 2005; Hanish, Martin, Fabes, & Barcelo, in press), a variation on social network analysis that can be used to describe numerous aspects of children's peer interactions, including their propensity to interact with dyads and groups. This method addresses some of the challenges to studying groups that are inherent in many social network techniques and yet retains the focus on the individual as the unit of analysis. Moreover, it offers a unique twist on conceptualizations of children's peer group involvement. It does not rely on a classification system, such as children classified as group members or isolates on the basis of their predominant peer relationships within the overall social structure of the classroom, as is often done with social network methods. Rather, the Q-connectivity method allows one to determine for each child the relative frequency of interaction with every possible peer or peer group—that is, the target child and every combination of peers. Thus, it is possible to calculate children's overall propensity to interact with peers as well as their relative exposure to particular peers or groups of peers (Hanish et al., in press). In this way, the full range of peer interactions for every child, even children who are relatively isolated in the classroom, can be studied.

Introduction to the Q-Connectivity Method

The Q-connectivity method is a mathematically derived variation on social network methods that can be used to model the dynamics of complex systems (Barcelo & Laubenbacher, 2005, 2006). The application of this method to the study of children's peer relationships rests on the idea that these relationships can be conceptualized as comprising complex patterns of discrete interactions with peers (Hinde & Stevenson-Hinde, 1987). The method provides a way to conceptualize and measure this complexity, which reflects the extensiveness of peer interactions and the frequency with which children are engaged with particular peers or groups of peers. This is made possible by using a parameter, Q, that represents the number of days children were observed to interact with peers and thereby reflects children's relative exposure to peers.

Two unique features of the Q-connectivity method are particularly relevant for the assessment of children's peer interactions: it permits the identification of each child's individual peer network, and it estimates the frequency (in this study, frequency is operationalized as number of days) with which each child affiliates with each peer or group of peers in the network (Hanish et al., in press). In this way, the compendium of interactions that a child has with every possible peer or possible group of peers can be identified and assessed, whether intensive and enduring or ephemeral and occasional. As applied to children's peer relationships, then, the Q-connectivity method makes it possible to examine the changing structure of individual children's interaction patterns with all available peers, such as classmates. Thus, this method makes it possible to estimate both within-child and between-child differences in patterns of peer interaction.

Given these qualities, Q-connectivity is a flexible method that can be used in many ways to study peer interactions and the socialization processes that occur within them. Because the relative frequency of exposure to every peer can be identified, it is possible to use this method to study both the breadth (the number of peers with whom each child interacts) and depth (the frequency with which each child interacts with every peer) of children's social structures. Breadth may be assessed, for example, by evaluating the extent to which children interact broadly with many peers or more selectively with just a few; depth may be assessed by examining how peer networks change at increasing levels of exposure (Hanish et al., in press).

Breadth and depth represent the most fundamental products of the Q-connectivity method and can be applied in diverse ways. For instance, breadth can be calculated in terms of dyadic interactions as well as group interactions, as we do in this chapter; breadth could be estimated for an entire sample of peers or for specific types of peers, such as same-sex peers or aggressive peers, and assessed at various levels of depth (exposure). Moreover, with this method, it is possible to incorporate estimates of children's own or peers' characteristics (for example, social competence, behavior, cognitive abilities, temperament), as well as indicators of interaction quality (for example, hostile versus cooperative) to assess children's social structures in more finely grained ways. In addition, the Q-connectivity method may be used to create moving temporal windows that can capture variations in peer structures across time. This would allow one to study, for instance, changes in children's breadth and depth over the course of an academic year or other period of time, or to assess the amount of time that passes between interactions with a particular peer or group of peers.

Using the Q-Connectivity Method to Study Preschoolers' Peer Group Interactions

In the research examined in this chapter, we apply the Q-connectivity method to study preschool children's tendencies to interact in groups of peers, defined as those that are at least triadic in size, that is, the target child plus two or more peers. We focus specifically on group interactions because they represent a particularly important social context for young children. The preschool period marks the shift from primarily solitary forms of play to increasing involvement in social activities and the dynamics of peer interactions (Fabes, Martin, & Hanish, in press). Social play is a relatively sophisticated activity that requires children to take others' perspectives, negotiate conflicts, regulate arousal, and behave prosocially, and group interactions are particularly challenging because children must consider the needs and desires of multiple peers.

With group interactions as a focus, we consider issues related to both breadth and depth. In regard to breadth, we are interested in the extent to which children interact with more than one peer triad, for example, a child may interact with peers 1 and 2 at one time and with peers 3 and 4 at another time. In regard to depth, we consider that some peer group interactions may be repeated over time, such that some children may have greater exposure to particular peer triads and less exposure to others, for example, multiple exposures to the triad consisting of peers 1 and 2 but only one interaction with the triad consisting of peers 3 and 4.

Assessment of Peer Group Interactions Using the Q-Connectivity Method. The Q-connectivity method permits the visualization of children's tendency to interact in groups as well as the computation of quantitative measures of group interactions. In this example, we relied on observational data obtained approximately two days per week over the course of the fall semester. The sample of children consisted of 183 preschoolers with complete data (53 percent boys; 68 percent Mexican American and 21 percent European American; mean age = 52 months, SD = 5 months) attending one of eleven Head Start classrooms in a southwestern metropolitan area. Data were collected across two waves. Ten-second observations were conducted by trained observers in the classrooms and on the playgrounds. For children who were present and available, observers recorded the identities of peers (up to five) who were observed in direct interaction (social conversation, rule-based play, or rough-and-tumble play, for example) or parallel play (say, playing alongside one another in the same activity) with the target child. (For details of the application of the observational procedures to the Q-connectivity method, see Hanish et al., in press.) All observations were entered into our Q-connectivity processing program, a Web-based data processing program.

One unique feature of the Q-connectivity method is that it represents children's social networks at the individual level rather than at the large group (for example, classroom) level. Thus, in this sample of 183 children, 183 sets of graphs, which visually depict children's social networks and serve as the basis for the calculation of quantitative measures, were produced, with each set of graphs representing an individual child's set of social networks across Q, the number of days of observation. For each child, Q graphs are produced where Q can vary from 1 to 58, the maximum number of assessments. In these data, observations were obtained on fifty-eight days for the wave 1 sample and on fifty days for the wave 2 sample; thus the maximum Q is 58 days.

As an example, the graph sequences for a target child, identified as girl 1, are illustrated in Figure 2.1. Girl 1 is not visually represented in the graphs; only her peers can be seen. The vertices represented in the first graph correspond to the peers who were observed to interact with girl 1 on at least one day during the semester (square vertices indicate male peers, and

Figure 2.1. Graphic Representation of Peer Interactions for Girl 1 as Frequency of Exposure to Peers Increases

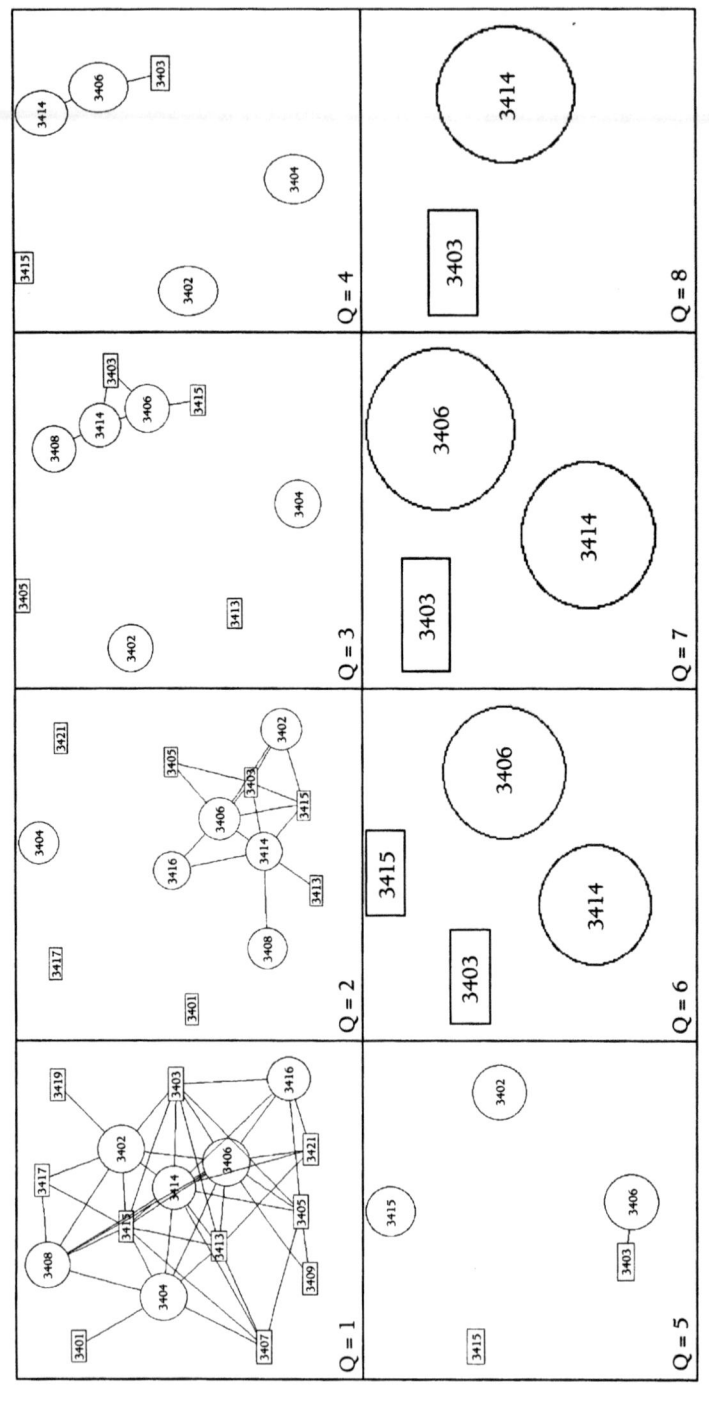

Note: As Q increases, frequency of exposure to peers increases. Q is operationalized as observation days; for example, the value of the group function at Q = 3 indicates with the same group of peers on at least three days of observation during the semester. Girl 1 was observed with no peers after Q vertices represent group interactions between the two indicated peers and the target child on at least Q days. Male peers are [f]emale peers with circular vertices.

circular vertices indicate female peers; the placement and size of the vertices on the graphs are arbitrary). Triadic groups are visually represented by the edges (lines) that connect two vertices. There is an edge between two vertices (that is, between two peers) if the two peers and girl 1 were seen interacting as a group on at least one day. Looking at the first graph, we see an edge between peers 3403 and 3406, indicating that the three children—girl 1, peer 3403, and peer 3406—interacted as a triad at least once. (It is possible that one or more of their group interactions included additional children as well. At this time, the size of the group beyond the triadic connection cannot be determined from the graphs; future enhancements to the Q-connectivity methodology are planned to address this issue.) The lack of an edge in the first graph connecting peers 3403 and 3419 indicates that these two children were never observed simultaneously with girl 1.

The subsequent graphs are constructed in a similar manner. For example, in the graph at $Q = 3$, the edges connecting peers 3403 and 3406 indicate that this group was observed to interact with girl 1 on at least three days. It is important to note that groups that were observed interacting on multiple days could have been observed on consecutive days, or the days could have been separated by several days, weeks, or even months. Thus, increases in Q reflect more frequent peer group interactions (greater exposure) with peers, but the length of time between interactions with the same peers is not consistent. Note also that at $Q = 6$ and beyond, no more edges are seen for girl 1, even though vertices appear in her graphs through $Q = 8$. This means that additional exposure to peers was dyadic; thus, although peers 3403 and 3406 both are seen in the $Q = 6$ graph, they did not interact with girl 1 as a group on six or more observational days.

Indicators of group interaction can be computed at each level of Q by counting the number of edges that connect the vertices within each graph. For instance, a count of the edges in graph 1 of Figure 2.1 indicates that girl 1 had exactly forty-six edges at $Q = 1$. This means that she engaged in group interactions in forty-six peer group triads on at least one occasion (in some cases, groups may have included more than two peers; thus, multiple triads may have been observed at the same time). At $Q = 4$, the presence of exactly two edges indicates that she interacted on at least four days with two of those peer group configurations, and the single edge at $Q = 5$ indicates that she was seen with one of those peer groups on five days. Thus, the data could be used in this way to represent variations in the number of groups with whom children interact. However, we can also use the data to study children's overall propensity to interact with peers beyond the dyadic level rather than the number of groups that make up their social landscape. Thus, for some subsequent analyses, these counts were aggregated to a dichotomous variable indicating absence versus presence of group interactions (0 versus 1 or more edges) at each level of Q.

Description of Preschoolers' Peer Group Interactions. We describe and interpret the data on children's group interactions in the light of the developmental level of our sample. In our sample of preschoolers, an

Table 2.1. Descriptive Statistics for Group Interactions

Q	M (SD)	Minimum	Maximum	No Group Interactions (%)
1	42.1 (26.3)	0	105	1
2	14.0 (14.8)	0	66	14
3	4.9 (7.5)	0	35	35
4	1.7 (3.2)	0	17	56
5	0.7 (1.5)	0	8	73
6	0.2 (0.7)	0	5	85
7	0.1 (0.5)	0	3	91
8	0.1 (0.3)	0	3	96
9	0.0 (0.2)	0	2	98
10	0.0 (0.2)	0	2	98
11	0.0 (0.1)	0	1	99

Note: Q indicates days. For example, the value of the group function at Q = 5 indicates that the target child interacted with the same group of peers on at least five days in the semester.

average of 44 percent of children's time was devoted to peer play, with the remaining time spent in solitary activities or interactions with the teacher. This distribution of young children's play time was normative and reflected young children's developing social skills. Of this, almost half of their peer play (48 percent, or 21 percent of their total time) consisted of play in groups larger than dyads. Thus, group interactions form an important part of preschoolers' social landscape.

The vast majority of children in this sample made forays into group interactions, and they did so with multiple peer group configurations. As depicted in Table 2.1 (in the Q = 1 row), only 1 percent of the children were never observed in a triadic interaction. Moreover, children's group interactions tended to incorporate numerous different configurations of peers. The Q = 1 row of Table 2.1 indicates that on average, preschoolers engaged forty-two peer group triads on at least one occasion (some of these groups may have included more than two peers; thus, multiple triads may have been observed simultaneously).

Despite preschoolers' general tendency to interact within groups of three or more, the percentage of children who interacted with the same group of peers on multiple occasions declined rapidly as Q increased (see Table 2.1). Fourteen percent of children were never observed with the same groups of peers on at least two occasions, 35 percent were never observed with the same groups of peers on at least three occasions, and 56 percent of children were never observed with the same groups of peers on at least four occasions. After Q = 11, no triadic interactions were observed. Two aspects of these data are particularly notable. First is the individual variation in triadic play. Although most young children were observed to engage with more than one peer, there were considerable individual differences in their tendency to maintain group interactions with the same peers. Second is the short duration of triadic play across all the children in the sample. These findings speak to the relative difficulty of sustaining group interactions across a period of time for young children and to individual differences in the ability to sustain interactions. Moreover, as Q increases, group interactions, for those children who maintain them, become increasingly selective. This can be seen in the rapid decrease in the mean number of group interactions from 42.1 at $Q = 1$ to 14.0 at $Q = 2$ to 1.7 at $Q = 4$ (see Table 2.1).

The Preschool Context: Group Interactions and Children's Early Learning

These findings reveal the complexity and developing sophistication of preschoolers' group interaction skills. To contextualize this, the preschool setting provides children with the opportunity to begin to practice group interactions. Indeed, for most children, preschool is their first opportunity to have extended contact with many different peers. Moreover, preschools are primarily designed to emphasize learning through play activities that often involve other children. In these play-based activities, children spend much of their time engaged in relatively unstructured activities that provide opportunities for peer interaction and form the backdrop of their early learning experiences and attitudes.

As the discussion illustrates, children's social and academic lives are inextricably intertwined. For instance, children's interactions and relationships with peers set the stage for engagement in learning and acquisition of knowledge (Ladd, Birch, & Buhs, 1999). Children who relate successfully with peers are more engaged in the school context and in academic tasks and participate more in classroom activities (Ladd, Herald, & Kochel, 2006). Thus, cognitive achievements such as literacy and math skills are thought to build on and may derive from social skills. From a developmental perspective, evidence suggests that experiences with peers are especially crucial influences on school adaptation early in elementary school, with studies suggesting that these social interactions contribute as much or more variance to early school-related outcomes as academic skills and family factors (Caprara, Barbaranelli, Pastorelli, Bandura, & Zimbardo, 2000).

Thus, in addition to describing young children's propensity to interact in groups, we use the Q-connectivity method to illustrate how preschoolers' patterns of group interaction relate to their early academic experiences, testing the hypothesis that propensity to interact in groups is related to literacy and math skills. Because the preschool period is a time when children begin to engage a larger social network of peers and because children's early academic functioning is critical to their overall later success and functioning (Ladd et al., 2006), finding a relation between young children's group interactions and academic functioning may suggest that early social experiences have long-term significance. In addition, we expect that this relation is moderated by children's own level of social skill. On the one hand, socially skilled children may be drawn to group interactions because they are well liked by many peers and because they possess the socioemotional skills that allow them to successfully negotiate complex peer interactions (Ladd et al., 2006). We would expect such children to benefit from opportunities to practice sophisticated social interaction skills, which might, in turn, be reflected in their academic performance. On the other hand, group interactions are not the sole domain of socially competent children. For instance, children who are aggressive may also form groups, but they tend to interact with other aggressive children (Cairns et al., 1988; Espelage, Holt, & Henkel, 2003). For these children, group interactions may be particularly disruptive and conflictual, and it may hinder successful academic learning rather than promote it. Thus, in the following analyses, we considered the possibility that group interactions confer different effects on learning depending on children's level of social competence, as measured by teachers' ratings on the Peer Interaction subscale of the Penn Interactive Peer Play Scale (Fantuzzo, Sutton-Smith, Coolahan, & Manz, 1995).

We conducted a set of multivariate analyses of variance (MANOVAs) to test whether children's propensity to interact in groups was associated with their early reading (letter and word identification and reading comprehension) and math (quantitative concepts) knowledge. To determine whether the relation between propensity to interact with groups (dichotomized as one or more group interactions versus none) varied by depth, we conducted the analyses separately for Q values of 2 through 6, with higher levels of Q indicating greater exposure to consistent groups of peers (analyses were not conducted at $Q = 1$ because of limited variability in the number of children who did not interact in groups, as shown in Table 2.1). Propensity to interact in groups was measured in the fall semester. At the end of the spring semester, children completed the Letter/Word Identification, Reading Comprehension, and Applied Math Problems subscales of the Woodcock-Johnson III (Woodcock, McGrew, & Mather, 2000) or the Batería-III Woodcock-Muñoz (Muñoz-Sandoval, Woodcock, McGrew, & Mather, 2005), depending on their preferred language (English or Spanish). We ran the analyses separately by sex because prior research has demonstrated robust sex differences in young boys' and girls' school adjustment (Fabes, Martin, Hanish, Anders, & Madden-Derdich, 2003; Fagot, 1985).

MANOVAs, controlling for children's age and the proportion of observation time in which they were unavailable for coding (due to school absence, being in the bathroom, napping, or something else), indicated that there were no main effects or interactions for boys' or girls' reading and math achievement at $Q = 2$ or $Q = 3$. However, significant group play by social competence interaction effects were evident for girls' reading comprehension and math skills at $Q = 4$ and above. At $Q = 4$ and $Q = 5$, there were significant univariate interaction effects on reading comprehension at $Q = 4$, $F(1, 64) = 3.87$, $p = .05$ and on mathematical abilities at $Q = 5$,

Figure 2.2. Social Competence as a Moderator of the Relation Between Group Play at Q = 4 and Reading Comprehension for Girls

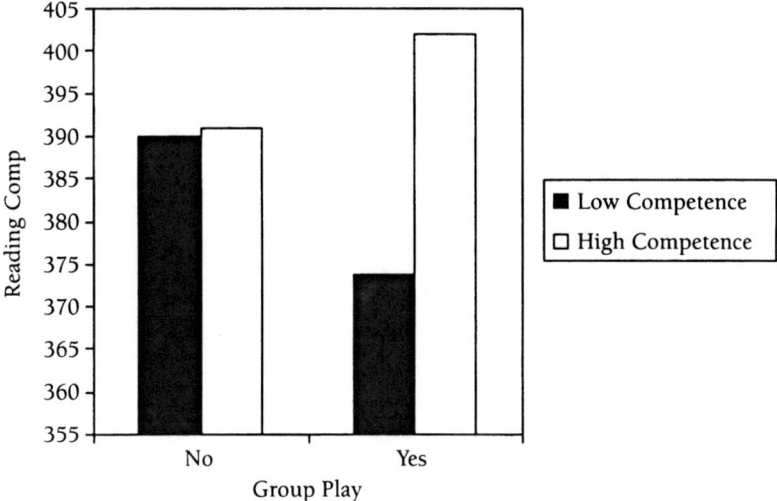

$F(1, 64) = 4.67$, $p < .05$. At Q = 6, the multivariate interaction effect was significant: $F(3, 62) = 2.85$, $p < .05$.

Further exploration of this pattern showed significant univariate effects on both reading comprehension and mathematical abilities, $F(1, 64) = 5.29$ and 6.10, $ps < .05$, respectively. The group play by social competence interaction on reading comprehension at Q = 4 is graphed in Figure 2.2. The simple effect for socially competent girls was marginally significant, $F(1, 40) = 3.83$, $p < .06$, but the simple effect for girls low in social competence did not reach significance. As illustrated, group play benefited socially competent girls through the relation with enhanced reading comprehension skills. The same pattern of effects at Q = 6 was obtained at a trend level. Socially competent girls who played in groups had higher reading comprehension scores than those who did not engage in group play, $F(1, 40) = 3.49$, $p < .07$. Figure 2.3 depicts the group play by social competence interaction on mathematical achievement at Q = 5. Here, the significant effect was seen for girls low in social competence, $F(1, 23) = 4.98$, $p < .05$. Girls who were less socially competent had significantly lower math scores than those who did not play in groups. The same pattern was seen at Q = 6, $F(1, 23) = 5.96$, $p < .05$. We conducted the same analyses a second time, adding children's prior receptive language ability, measured for English speakers with the Peabody Picture Vocabulary Test (Dunn & Dunn, 1997) and for Spanish speakers with the Test de Vocabulario en Imagenes Peabody as a covariate. The pattern of findings was similar.

Figure 2.3. Social Competence as a Moderator of the Relation Between Group Play at Q = 5 and Mathematics Achievement for Girls

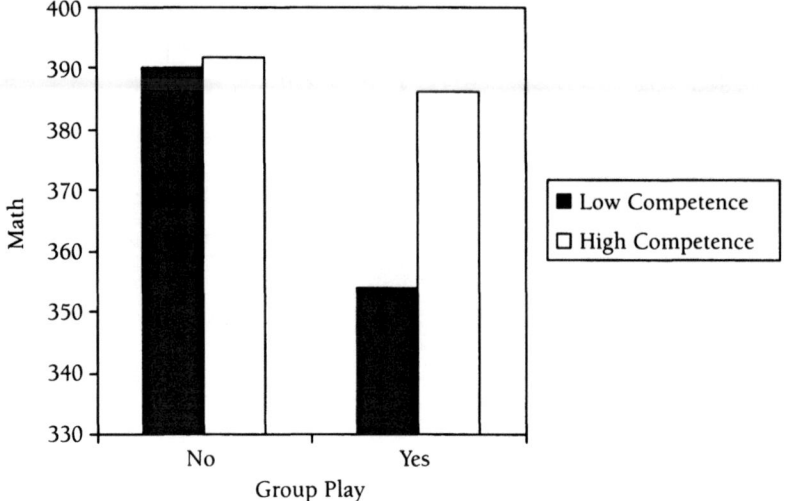

Less evidence was obtained for the idea that boys' triadic play was associated with their early academic achievement. There was a marginally significant multivariate effect for the group play by social competence interaction at Q = 5, $F(3, 73) = 2.61$, $p < .06$. Examination of the univariate findings revealed a significant group play by social competence interaction for the ability to identify letters and words, $F(1, 75) = 4.90$, $p < .05$. The pattern of findings parallels that seen for girls. That is, group play was associated with marginally higher reading achievement scores for socially competent boys, $F(1, 24) = 3.46$, $p < .08$. No other significant main or interaction effects were found for group play on boys' early academic achievement.

These findings highlight the importance of triadic group play to young children's, particularly young girls', early academic skills, and they suggest that being able to sustain group play successfully is strongly related to outcomes (effects were obtained at higher Q levels), with this effect moderated by social competence. Socially competent girls who played frequently in groups fared well academically—as well as, or better than, their peers who did not play in groups. However, incompetent girls who played frequently in groups were hindered in academic skills by their group play. Several interpretations can be made of these findings. Perhaps low socially competent girls who play in groups do so with other girls who are similarly low in social competence. As a result, their group interactions may not be conducive to learning academic-related skills. Alternatively, perhaps these girls are overwhelmed by the larger group size; because of their limited social skills, they may become easily stressed by the demands of maintaining group play. Increased stress might then interfere with the learning process.

Although little attention has been paid to the ways in which preschoolers' peer interactions relate to their school readiness, studies with older children suggest some ways in which peer relationships at school might facilitate or hinder knowledge acquisition in many domains, including mathematical explorations and concept learning (Saxe, Guberman, & Gearhart, 1987) and language and literacy (Kumpulainen & Mutanen, 2000). Participation in classroom activities is a social process through which children teach and are taught by peers; through these exchanges, children learn about themselves, their partners, and the activity in which they are engaged, such as the curriculum. Shared experiences with peers in which children jointly and collaboratively solve problems and structure activities have been found to promote cognitive growth and motivation (Guay, Boivin, & Hodges, 1999). Peers may exert influence by encouraging, discouraging, or ignoring certain behaviors; providing direct instruction; or helping others (Chambers, 1995). Positive peer interactions, as is the case for socially competent children, generates support for learning (Caprara et al., 2000). In contrast, negative and conflict-ridden peer interactions, which characterize the relationships of less competent children, relate to disaffection and disengagement in school, the earliest predictors of children's declining performance and eventual school dropout (Ladd et al., 1999). These mechanisms are likely explanations for the effects that consistent group play (with the same peers) has on early achievement. However, it is important to note that the studies cited here have focused generally on interactions with any peers rather than consistent group-based interactions with the same set of peers. It is intriguing that our findings suggest that consistency is important. Perhaps more complex and sophisticated interactions occur over time within peer groups that may be particularly amenable to enhancing children's school-related skills. Further research is needed to explore the directionality of the findings and to explore how and why peer group exposure relates to academic outcomes for girls.

That the effects were stronger for girls than for boys is consistent with the findings of previous studies that have identified different patterns of predictors of early school readiness for boys and for girls (Fabes, Martin, Hanish, & Moss, 2006). For instance, skills and behaviors that directly influence both social and academic skills, such as communication skills, have been shown to be important predictors of young girls', but not young boys', school readiness; in contrast, boys' abilities to effectively regulate their behaviors and attention seem particularly critical to their early learning experiences. Because girls' play styles tend to be verbally based (Maccoby, 1998), the ability to engage in group play with the same group over time may represent a particularly sophisticated interaction style, which then affects opportunities for learning, at least for girls who are less socially competent. For boys, however, group play is less likely to rely on sophisticated verbal skills and more likely to rely on active play styles. Thus, boys' group play may provide fewer opportunities to learn the skills needed for literacy or math learning. Rather, the group context may confer different effects on boys' learning, such as enhanced school engagement and interest.

Conclusion

We introduced the Q-connectivity method for studying children's peer interactions and applied it to study preschoolers' involvement with groups of peers. We demonstrated how the method can provide information on individual differences in children's propensity to engage in groups and their tendency to engage with the same groups over time. We also showed that the method can be used to draw insights about development—in this example, children's early academic skills. Although it is beyond the scope of this chapter, the Q-connectivity method has the potential to offer a host of informative measures of interactional patterns above and beyond breadth and depth; density, maximum value of Q, and a variety of vector measures across Q are examples of just a few measures that can be calculated using this variation on social network methods. Moreover, because the data obtained using this technique can be easily integrated into statistical procedures that use the individual as the unit of analysis, they are readily used by social scientists. In summary, the Q-connectivity method offers an expanded ability to assess peer interactions and thus has the potential to inform researchers about peer socialization processes.

References

Barcelo, H., & Laubenbacher, R. (2005). Perspectives on a homotopy theory and its applications. *Journal of Discrete Mathematics, 298,* 39–61.

Barcelo, H., & Laubenbacher, R. (2006). *Graph theoretic tools for dynamic network analysis.* Manuscript submitted for publication.

Cairns, R. B., Cairns, B. D., Neckerman, H. J., Gest, S. D., & Gariepy, J. L. (1988). Social networks and aggressive behavior: Peer support or peer rejection? *Developmental Psychology, 24*(6), 815–823.

Caprara, G. V., Barbaranelli, C., Pastorelli, C., Bandura, A., & Zimbardo, P. G. (2000). Prosocial foundations of children's academic achievement. *Psychological Science, 11,* 302–306.

Chambers, S. M. (1995). Age, prior opinions, and peer interactions in opinion restructuring. *Child Development, 66,* 178–192.

Dunn, L. M., & Dunn, L. M. (1997). *Examiner's manual for the Peabody Picture Vocabulary Test Third Edition.* Circle Pines, MN: American Guidance Services.

Espelage, D. L., Holt, M. K., & Henkel, R. R. (2003). Examination of peer-group contextual effects on aggression during early adolescence. *Child Development, 74*(1), 205–220.

Fabes, R. A., Martin, C. L., & Hanish, L. D. (in press). Children's behaviors and interactions with peers. In W.B.K. Rubin & B. Larsen (Eds.), *Handbook of peer interactions, relationships, and groups.* New York: Guilford Press.

Fabes, R. A., Martin, C. L., Hanish, L. D., Anders, M. C., & Madden-Derdich, D. A. (2003). Early school competence: The roles of sex-segregated play and effortful control. *Developmental Psychology, 39*(5), 848–858.

Fabes, R. A., Martin, C. L., Hanish, L. D., & Moss, A. (2006). *Teachers' perceptions of adjustment to kindergarten: The role of young children's attentional abilities*. Manuscript submitted for publication.

Fagot, B. I. (1985). Beyond the reinforcement principle: Another step toward understanding sex role development. *Developmental Psychology, 21*, 1097–1104.

Fantuzzo, J. W., Sutton-Smith, B., Coolahan, K. C., & Manz, P. H. (1995). Assessment of preschool play interaction behaviors in young low-income children: Penn interactive peer play scale. *Early Childhood Research Quarterly, 10*, 105–120.

Guay, F., Boivin, M., & Hodges, E.V.E. (1999). Predicting change in academic achievement: A model of peer experiences and self-system processes. *Journal of Educational Psychology, 91*, 105–115.

Hanish, L. D., Martin, C. L., Fabes, R. A., & Barcelo, H. (in press). The breadth of peer relationships among preschoolers: An application of the Q-connectivity method to externalizing behavior. *Child Development*.

Hinde, R. A., & Stevenson-Hinde, J. (1987). Interpersonal relationships and child development. *Developmental Review, 7*(1), 1–21.

Kindermann, T. A. (1993). Natural peer groups as contexts for individual development: The case of children's motivation in school. *Developmental Psychology, 29*, 970–977.

Kumpulainen, K., & Mutanen, M. (2000). Mapping the dynamics of peer group interaction: A method of analysis of social shared learning processes. In H. Cowie & G.v.d. Aalsvoort (Eds.), *Advances in learning and instruction series. Social interaction in learning and instruction: The meaning of discourse for the construction of knowledge* (pp. 144–160). New York: Pergamon/Elsevier Science.

Ladd, G. W., Birch, S. H., & Buhs, E. (1999). Children's social and scholastic lives in kindergarten: Related spheres of influence? *Child Development, 70*, 1373–1400.

Ladd, G. W., Herald, S. L., & Kochel, K. P. (2006). School readiness: Are there social prerequisites? *Early Education and Development, 17*(1), 115–150.

Maccoby, E. E. (1998). *The two sexes: Growing up apart, coming together*. Cambridge, MA: Harvard University Press.

Muñoz-Sandoval, A. F., Woodcock, R. W., McGrew, K. S., & Mather, K. (2005). *Bateria III Woodcock-Muñoz*. Itasca, IL: Riverside Publishing.

Richards, W. D., & Rice, R. E. (1981). The NEGOPY network analysis program. *Social Networks, 3*, 215–223.

Saxe, G. B., Guberman, S. R., & Gearhart, M. (1987). Social processes in early number development. *Monographs of the Society for Research in Child Development, 52* (2, Serial No. 216).

Woodcock, R. W., McGrew, K. S., & Mather, K. (2000). *Woodcock-Johnson III*. Itasca, IL: Riverside Publishing.

LAURA D. HANISH is an associate professor of child development in the School of Social and Family Dynamics, Program in Family and Human Development, at Arizona State University in Tempe, Arizona.

HÉLÈNE BARCELO is a professor in the Department of Mathematics and Statistics at Arizona State University in Tempe, Arizona.

CAROL LYNN MARTIN is a Cowden Distinguished Professor of child development in the School of Social and Family Dynamics, Program in Human Development, at Arizona State University in Tempe, Arizona.

RICHARD A. FABES is the Dee and John Whiteman Distinguished Professor of child development and the founding director of the School of Social and Family Dynamics at Arizona State University in Tempe, Arizona.

JENNIFER HOLMWALL is a doctoral student and instructor in the Department of Mathematics and Statistics, at Arizona State University, in Tempe, Arizona.

FRANCISCO PALERMO is a doctoral candidate in the School of Social and Family Dynamics, Program in Family and Human Development, at Arizona State University in Tempe, Arizona.

How are African American and European American children getting along in integrated elementary schools? The authors find substantial integration in majority black and multicultural classrooms, but ethnic segregation and cross-ethnic antipathies are more common in majority white classrooms.

Social Integration Between African American and European American Children in Majority Black, Majority White, and Multicultural Elementary Classrooms

Philip C. Rodkin, Travis Wilson, Hai-Jeong Ahn

The racial and ethnic composition of American classrooms is once again under scrutiny. The ideal of the integrated school is under challenge in the face of resegregation (Graham, 2007; Schofield & Hausman, 2004) and the divided U.S. Supreme Court decision in *Parents Involved in Community Schools v. Seattle School District, No. 1* (2007), in which voluntary municipal efforts to promote integration were struck down. In the course of this debate, questions have arisen as to whether it matters that American classrooms are integrated (Williams, 2007). As Graham (2007) tells it, the U.S. Commission on Civil Rights (2006) placed integrated schools low on the list of factors that promote children's social and academic growth. Columnist David Brooks (2007, July 6) comments that black and white students "do not go to the same schools. And when they do go to the same schools, they do not lead shared lives. . . . If you separate people into different

---

This research was supported by grants to P.C.R. from the National Institute of Child Health and Human Development (R03 HD48491–01) and the Spencer Foundation (Small Grant 20050079). We thank the children, teachers, and school principals who participated in and contributed to this project.

groups—no matter how arbitrary the basis of the distinction—they will quickly begin discriminating against others they deem unlike themselves." There is basis in the minimal group paradigm (Tajfel, 1970) to what Brooks says, but does this sorry state of affairs hold as an inevitability, unaffected by the characteristics of particular children and schools?

During this time that the integrated classroom is being passed over as unworkable or without impact, psychological evidence has emerged suggesting that classroom social organization and climate influences children's development. Child-by-environment models highlight peer experiences such as rejection and acceptance that necessarily transpire within social settings (Ladd, 2005). Classroom norms, ethnic composition, and teacher styles affect the social status children accord to aggression (Chang, 2004) and how children adjust to being harassed (Bellmore, Witkow, Graham, & Juvonen, 2004; Hanish & Guerra, 2000). The unfortunate irony is that children's classroom environments are being downplayed in policy circles while empirical studies demonstrate the value of working with the fundamental settings, like schools and classrooms, in which children grow (Tseng & Seidman, 2007).

In this chapter, we use social network analysis and multilevel modeling to examine a central feature of classroom social organization: the ethnic composition of the classroom. We examine classroom ethnic composition as it relates to patterns of social integration between African American and European American children. Developmental psychologists began studying children's intergroup relations as soon as investigative tools became available. In the time of Moreno (1934), there was interest in topics such as "racial cleavage" (Criswell, 1937) and interracial nominations of social preference (Clark & Clark, 1947); these works had an impact on the Supreme Court's use of psychological evidence in *Brown v. Board of Education of Topeka* (1954). Today, advances in sociometric and social network technology offer researchers much greater precision in analyzing still-relevant questions regarding children's intergroup relations at school.

We asked whether the social integration patterns of black and white students vary according to whether their classroom has a clear ethnic majority and, if so, whether the numerically preponderant group is African American or European American. We hypothesized that integration patterns within majority black and majority white classrooms would depend on children's status as a numerical majority or minority in the classroom and also on minority status in the macrosystemic culture. As such, a white student in a majority black classroom should have different integration patterns from a black student in a majority white classroom.

There is no clear answer to the question of whether African American and European American children are equally likely to have segregated peer relationships, even apart from interactions with classroom context. As Aboud, Mendelson, and Purdy (2003) noted, in some studies black children are found to segregate more (Criswell, 1937; Hallinan, 1982; Quillian &

Campbell, 2003), but others find greater same-race preferences on the part of white children (Dubois & Hirsch, 1990) or even substantial positive intergroup contact (Singleton & Asher, 1979).

Studies also conflict when it comes to the question of whether social integration patterns for African American and European American children differ by classroom ethnic composition. Are African American children more likely to have segregated friendships in majority white classrooms, a case in which African Americans are a "double minority" (Kistner, Metzler, Gatlin, & Risi, 1993)? In pursuit of this question, Hallinan (1982) investigated friendship choices among white and black fourth through seventh graders in twenty northern California classrooms that were majority white (approximately 75 percent), majority black (approximately 75 percent), or racially balanced. Hallinan (1982) found that the general tendency for African American students to have more exclusively same-ethnic friendships was mitigated in majority white classrooms, where greater integration was the norm. Jackson, Barth, Powell, and Lochman (2006) surveyed fifty-nine fifth-grade classrooms and asked children whom they liked most and least. They found that African American children received more liked most and fewer liked least nominations when there were more African Americans in their classroom; in contrast, ratings for white children were similar across classrooms. Jackson et al.'s results (2006) cannot be easily reconciled with the greater integration in majority white classrooms that Hallinan (1982) reported a generation ago. Still other studies find no interaction between individual ethnicity and classroom ethnic majority (Kistner et al., 1993; Lease & Blake, 2005). Taken together, it is hard to predict from previous literature how patterns of social integration between African American and European American students differ across classroom contexts. However, like Hallinan (1982) and Jackson et al. (2006), we expect an interaction between individual ethnicity and classroom ethnic majority.

We also anticipated that social integration would be greatest for both African American and European American children in multicultural classrooms in which there are many ethnic groups and no clear majority (Hamm, Brown, & Heck, 2005; Juvonen, Nishina, & Graham, 2006; Quillian & Campbell, 2003). However, the benefits of diversity remain an open question in relation to children's social integration. Some have found that in diverse schools, same-ethnicity cliques can emerge as the social ecology balkanizes (Hallinan, 1982; Moody, 2001).

In previous studies, segregation has been determined on the basis of one or two peer relationship measures: friendships and nominations for likes most and likes least. Reciprocation (for example, p likes o and o likes p) is often not a criterion for these measures, although lack of reciprocation does not distinguish actual relationships from unrequited sentiment. In this study, patterns of integration and segregation are determined across four relationships, with three (group affiliates being the exception) involving reciprocation:

- *Friendships.* Children's friendships are a classic measure of peer relations; most research on children's intergroup relations uses cross-ethnic friendships as an outcome (Aboud et al., 2003; Lease & Blake, 2005; Hallinan, 1982; Moody, 2001).
- *Peer group affiliates.* Why might there be differences between children's friends and their group affiliates? Friendships imply greater intimacy and closeness than a group of children who regularly interact. We used social cognitive mapping (Cairns, Xie, & Leung, 1998; Gest, Graham-Bermann, & Hartup, 2001) to generate affiliative groups from unreciprocated multi-informant data where children name their peer group and also groups to which they do not belong.
- *Mutual liking.* Asher, Parker, and Walker (1996) distinguish acceptance (the proportion of peers naming a child as "liked most") and friendships. Singleton and Asher (1979) suggest that their use of a rating scale of liking ("How much do you like to play with [this person] at school?") rather than friendships may explain their unique findings of cross-race acceptance in integrated elementary schools. Kistner et al. (1993) and Jackson et al. (2006) examined unreciprocated sentiments of liked most and least.
- *Mutual disliking (antipathy).* In the absence of positive intergroup sentiment, the distribution of antipathies helps distinguish two scenarios: one where groups ignore one another versus a second where they harbor active hostility. For instance, Rodkin, Pearl, Farmer, and Van Acker (2003) found in a longitudinal sample of third through fifth graders that boys and girls had almost as many cross-sex as same-sex liked-least nominations, a striking contrast to the absence of cross-sex nominations in positive sentiments. Boys and girls appeared to participate actively in relationships of mutual dislike. In this study, we pose a similar question regarding mutual antipathies between European American and African American children.

There are three additional methodological strengths of this study. First, our sample of third and fourth graders is divided relatively equally into majority black, majority white, and multicultural classrooms. In majority white and black classrooms, approximately one-third of students are in the numerical minority, enough to allow for reliable analysis. Second, we apply a compositionally invariant segregation index to peer relations measures to control for baseline differences in the availability of same- and cross-ethnicity peers. Finally, we use multi-level modeling to disentangle nested effects of individual ethnicity and classroom ethnic composition. Through these procedures, we hope to shed new light on whether classroom ethnic composition makes a difference in the social integration patterns of African American and European American children.

Method

In this section, we describe the participants, survey measures, and procedures used to generate our indexes of segregation.

Participants. In our sample were thirty-two third- and fourth-grade classrooms within nine schools across three midwestern school districts. The 720 children in these classrooms were diverse: 43 percent African American, 43 percent European American, 3 percent Latino/a, 8 percent Asian, and 3 percent other. Children were about equally likely to be enrolled in classrooms that were majority African American, majority European American, and multicultural (no clear ethnic majority and in many classrooms a strong Latino and/or Asian minority). Table 3.1 shows that the average ethnic compositions of majority black and majority white classrooms were virtually symmetrical, with 60 percent of children in the ethnic majority, 33 to 34 percent in the ethnic minority, and 5 to 10 percent with Latino, Asian, or other backgrounds. Majority black, majority white, and multicultural classrooms were each dispersed across five out of the nine sampled schools. Of the 720 students, 76 percent participated (N = 547). Participants were representative of the ethnic composition of the larger sample within each classroom type ($p > .4$). There were 180 participating children (81 boys, 99 girls) in the ten majority black classrooms, 194 (93 boys, 101 girls) in the eleven majority white classrooms, and 173 (83 boys, 90 girls) in the eleven multicultural classrooms. There was a trend toward participation rate differences by classroom composition

Table 3.1. Distribution of Children in Majority Black, Majority White, and Multicultural Classrooms

Classroom Ethnic Composition	Classrooms	Percentage of Children				
		Black	White	Latino	Asian	Other
Majority black	10	60.9 (8.6)	34.0 (6.6)	1.7 (3.1)	1.3 (3.6)	2.1 (3.7)
Majority white	11	33.1 (9.3)	60.2 (6.0)	1.3 (3.9)	4.2 (4.0)	1.3 (3.9)
Multicultural	11	34.2 (13.6)	33.7 (10.7)	5.3 (4.6)	19.1 (14.4)	7.7 (5.6)
Total	32	42.6 (16.3)	42.5 (15.1)	2.8 (4.3)	8.3 (11.6)	3.8 (5.2)

Note: Standard deviations are in parentheses.

($F(2,29) = 3.17$, $p = 0.057$): 76 percent participation in majority black, 82 percent in majority white, and 70 percent in multicultural classrooms.

Sociometric Survey. We surveyed participants in the spring semester of 2005. One researcher read aloud the survey as at least two others walked around the classroom to monitor students' progress and answer questions. The study drew on four sociometric items:

- *Friendship.* Children were asked to circle yes or no to the question, "Some kids have a number of close friends, but others have just one best friend and still others don't have a best friend. What about you? Do you have a best friend?" Children responding affirmatively were prompted to write the names of up to six children whom they considered to be their best friends. Reciprocated friendships were considered for analysis.
- *Peer group affiliations* (social cognitive mapping). Children were asked to circle yes or no to the question, "Do you hang around together a lot with some kids in your classroom?" Participants responding affirmatively were prompted to check off boxes adjacent to the first names and last initials of peers in their classroom under the heading: "MY GROUP." Immediately following the "MY GROUP" question, children were asked, "Besides the group that you're in, are there other kids in your classroom who hang around together a lot?" Children responding affirmatively were prompted to write the first names and last initials of every child in each group they could think of.
- *Likes most.* Children were asked to check off boxes adjacent to the first names and last initials of peers in their classroom who best fit the description of "kids who I would LIKE MOST to play with," using an unlimited nomination procedure (children could check off as many names as they felt appropriate). Only reciprocated nominations were considered.
- *Likes least.* Children were asked to check off boxes adjacent to the first names and last initials of peers in their classroom who best fit the description of "kids who I would LIKE LEAST to play with," using unlimited nominations. We considered only reciprocated nominations, or mutual antipathies.

Calculating Ethnic Segregation and Integration. We were interested in tendencies toward segregation for each of the four measures of peer relationships. To assess segregation, we used the compositionally invariant odds-ratio, $\log \alpha$, which controls for opportunities present for same- and cross-ethnic contact in classrooms of varying ethnic composition (Moody, 2001). Measures of segregation that do not maintain compositional invariance yield misleading results (Gorard & Taylor, 2002).

We calculated $\log \alpha$ for each of the four sociometric measures for each African American and European American participant. We could not consider Latino, Asian, or children of other ethnicities due to low sample size. We created an ethnicity-by-nominations cross-tabulation, where $\log \alpha = \log (AD/BC)$ in Table 3.2. In this table, A is the number of same-ethnic ties, B

Table 3.2. Calculating Compositionally Invariant Segregation Indexes

	Same-Ethnic Dyad	Cross-Ethnic Dyad
Tie	A	B
No tie	C	D

is the number of cross-ethnic ties, C is the number of same-ethnic peers with whom the child does not have ties, and D is the number of cross-ethnic peers with whom the child does not have ties. In all cases, we are limited to consider only ties between African American and European American children.

Consider a classroom that has twenty-four students with the following ethnic distribution: fifteen black (62.5 percent), seven white (29.2 percent), and two Asian (8.3 percent). A black male student in this classroom has friendships with two black classmates (A = 2; C = 12) and one white classmate (B = 1; D = 6). Thus, log α = log (AD/BC) = log $[(2 \times 6)/(1 \times 12)]$ = log (1.0) = 0. The zero value indicates that the child exhibits no same- or cross-ethnic preference given the ethnic composition of his class. Now consider a second example. A black female student in the same class has three black friends (A = 3; C = 11) and one white friend (B = 1; D = 6). For her, log α = log $[(3 \times 6)/(1 \times 11)]$ = log (1.64) = +0.21. The small positive value denotes that she is slightly more likely to have same- than cross-ethnicity friendships. In contrast, a black student with two black and two white friends has a log α of –0.39, reflecting a tendency toward cross-ethnicity friendships.

The logarithmic scale is interpreted as follows: 0 indicates no preference, positive values indicate same-ethnicity segregation, and negative values indicate cross-ethnicity integration. We inverted the odds ratio for antipathies so that positive values mean cross-ethnic antipathies and negative values same-ethnic antipathies. The larger the absolute value of log α, the greater the effect is. Every African American and European American participant had four log α indexes corresponding to ethnic segregation in his or her patterns of reciprocated friendships, peer group affiliations, and reciprocated liked-most and liked-least sentiments.

We obtained mean differences between African American and European Americans on the segregation indexes (log α), even though three of our four outcome measures required reciprocation. Figure 3.1 illustrates how students of one ethnicity can have higher segregation indexes than students of the other ethnicity even under conditions of reciprocation. It shows a classroom of fourteen children, composed of nine white (64.3 percent) and five black students (35.7 percent), networked by friendship. Gray nodes depict African American children, and black nodes depict European American children; adjacent to each node is the segregation index for each child. Students

Figure 3.1. Example Sociogram of Friendship Segregation by Ethnicity

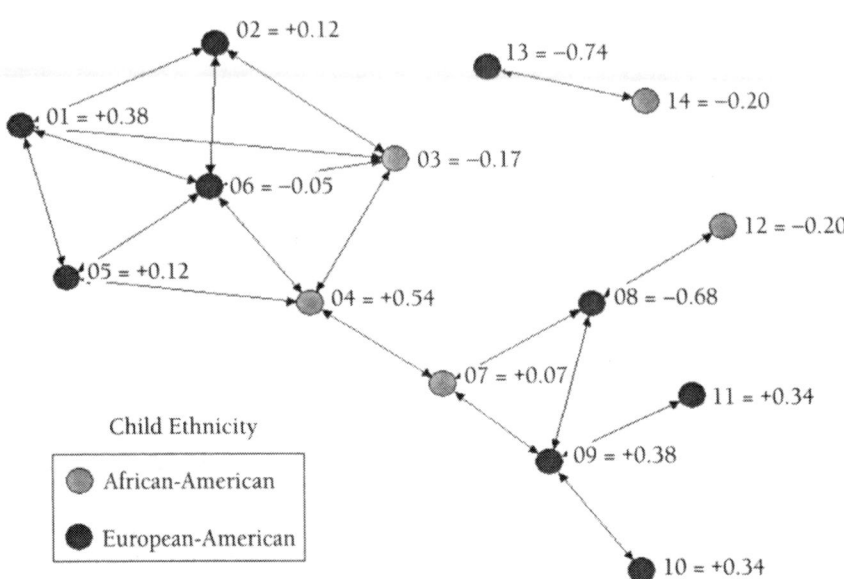

13 (a European American) and 14 (an African American) form a dyad and have ties only with each other. Both have negative segregation indexes, indicating cross-ethnic integration. Student 13's index (log α = –0.74) is more negative than student 14's (log α = –0.20) because student 13 has fewer cross-ethnic peers from which to choose; greater weight is given to student 13's cross-ethnic tie given that African Americans are the minority in this classroom. Students 4 (log α = +0.54) and 6 (log α = –0.05), members of a prominent clique with six students, reveal a more dramatic contrast. Student 4 evidences strong segregation tendencies, whereas student 6 has a slight pattern toward integration. This difference arises because student 4 has ties with 50 percent of her same-ethnic peers and just 22 percent of her cross-ethnic peers, whereas student 6 has ties with 38 percent of her same-ethnic peers and as many as 40 percent of her cross-ethnic peers.

An individual's segregation index accounts for all persons to whom one is connected while being sensitive to differences in opportunities for same- and cross-ethnic ties. African American and European American children in the same classroom can have different means on the segregation indexes despite the mutuality criterion of friendship, liked most, and liked least measures.

Multilevel Models. Multilevel modeling (hierarchical linear modeling program, version 6.01) was used to determine whether patterns of social

Table 3.3. Correlations Between Individual Segregation Indexes for Mutual Friendships, Peer Groups, Mutual Liking, and (Inverted) Mutual Disliking

	1	2	3	4
1. Mutual friendships	—	+0.50 (290)	+0.63 (289)	+0.10 (251)
2. Peer groups	—	—	+0.50 (366)	+0.20 (332)
3. Mutual liking	—	—	—	+0.23 (315)
4. Mutual disliking	—	—	—	—

Note: Numbers of students are in parentheses; these vary because some students may have one type of relationship but not another.

segregation and integration were associated with (1) individual ethnicity, (2) classroom ethnic composition, and (3) the interaction between individual ethnicity and classroom ethnic composition. We followed the procedures of Rodkin, Farmer, Pearl, and Van Acker (2006) in constructing four multilevel models, one for each outcome: friendship segregation, peer group segregation, liked-most segregation, and liked-least integration. Table 3.3 shows that segregation in friendships, group affiliations, and mutual liking were strongly correlated with rs ranging from +0.50 to +0.63. Integration scores for antipathies were weakly but positively correlated with segregation for the positive peer relations measures ($rs < +0.25$). Initial modeling indicated that gender was not a significant factor, so we excluded gender from final models. Therefore, each model had the following independent variables: ethnicity (level 1), coding African American +1 and European-American –1, and classroom ethnic composition (level 2), coded by two orthogonal dummy variables:

Classroom Distribution	Classroom Majority	Multicultural
Majority white	–1	–0.5
Majority black	+1	–0.5
Multicultural	0	+1

All models have this structure:

Level 1: $Y_{ij} = \beta_{0j} + \beta_{1j}\text{ETHNICITY} + r_{ij}$
Level 2a: $\beta_{0j} = \gamma_{00} + \gamma_{01}\text{CMAJ} + \gamma_{02}\text{MC} + u_{0j}$
Level 2b: $\beta_{1j} = \gamma_{10} + \gamma_{11}\text{CMAJ} + \gamma_{12}\text{MC} + u_{1j}$

The level 1 equation, including individual ethnicity, examines whether European American or African American students are more likely to have same-ethnicity friendships and peer groups and to have reciprocated nominations of like most and (inverted) like least with same-ethnicity peers. This helps answer the question: Do European American or African American children have a higher rate of same-ethnicity positive social ties and cross-ethnicity negative ties?

The level 2a equation examines the importance of classroom ethnic distributions on children's tendency to participate in segregated peer relationships, regardless of individual ethnicity. When placed at the intercept (level 2a), the classroom majority variable (CMAJ) indexes whether segregation is more likely depending on who—European Americans or African Americans—is in the numerical majority. The multicultural variable (MC) indexes whether ethnically diverse classrooms have less (or more) segregation than classrooms in which a clear numerical majority exists.

The level 2b equation accounts for cross-level interactions between individual ethnicity (level 1) and classroom ethnic distribution (level 2). The γ_{11} effect compares the experiences of classroom minority group and majority group members in majority black and majority white classrooms. We were particularly interested in possible asymmetries between the integration patterns of African American and European American children as classroom minorities. The γ_{12} effect represents the interaction between ethnicity and multicultural classrooms and indexes whether multicultural classroom contexts operate similarly for African American and European American children's social integration patterns.

Results

Table 3.4 presents results for the four multilevel models predicting ethnic segregation in mutual friendships, peer group affiliations, mutual liking, and mutual disliking. In the first three models, there were consistent, significant effects for the intercept (γ_{00} is positive, indicating same-ethnicity preferences), child ethnicity (γ_{10} is positive, indicating greater segregation among African American students), and the interaction of child ethnicity and classroom majority (γ_{11} is negative, indicating that African American segregation is highest in majority white classrooms). In the last model for mutual dislike, γ coefficients were significant and positive for the intercept (indicating more cross-ethnicity antipathies overall), negative for classroom majority (indicating more cross-ethnicity antipathies in majority white classrooms), and positive for the interaction of child ethnicity and classroom majority (indicating more cross-race antipathies among whites in majority white classrooms). In no case was there an effect involving multicultural classrooms. The four models are discussed below in detail.

Friendship Segregation. We found three significant effects in the model for children's friendship segregation: (1) the intercept (γ_{00} = +0.23),

Table 3.4. Segregation in Mutual Friendships, Peer Groups, Mutual Liking, and Mutual Disliking by Child Ethnicity and Classroom Ethnic Composition

	Segregation Index											
	Mutual Friendship			Peer Group			Mutual Liking			Mutual Disliking		
Fixed Effect Coefficient	Effect	SE	t (25)	Effect	SE	t (29)	Effect	SE	t (27)	Effect	SE	t (27)
Intercept (γ_{00})	+0.227	.066	3.46**	+0.429	.073	5.85***	+0.350	.053	6.55***	+0.136	.059	2.33*
Child ethnicity (γ_{10})	+0.210	.045	4.69***	+0.131	.034	3.81***	+0.105	.047	2.25*	+0.015	.041	0.36
Classroom majority (γ_{01})	−0.041	.072	−0.57	−0.040	.102	−0.39	−0.107	.063	−1.69	−0.155	.069	−2.24*
Ethnicity × CMAJ (γ_{11})	−0.125	.044	−2.83**	−0.161	.043	−3.79***	−0.177	.063	−2.80**	+0.129	.044	2.96**
Multicultural (γ_{02})	−0.052	.107	−0.49	−0.081	.090	−0.90	−0.021	.077	−0.27	−0.008	.084	−0.10
Ethnicity × MC (γ_{12})	+0.115	.076	1.51	+0.013	.048	0.26	−0.084	.050	−1.68	+0.015	.067	0.23

Note: Values for the γ parameters listed in parentheses in column 1 are presented in the four effect columns, followed by standard errors and t-values. In the multilevel model, child ethnicity was entered at level 1 and classroom majority (CMAJ) and multicultural (MC) at level 2 at the intercept (γ_{01}, γ_{02}) and child ethnicity slope (γ_{11}, γ_{12}). Segregation values for mutual disliking are inverted, so positive effects indicate more cross-ethnic antipathies.

* $p < .05$. ** $p < .01$. *** $p < .001$.

(2) a main effect for individual ethnicity (γ_{10} = +0.21), and (3) an interaction between individual ethnicity and classroom majority (γ_{11} = –0.13). Figure 3.2 illustrates these effects, with the individual segregation index (log α) plotted along the ordinate and the three classroom compositions (majority black, majority white, and multicultural) plotted along the abscissa. For each classroom type, average friendship segregation indexes are displayed for African American and European American children. The horizontal line corresponding to the intercept or grand mean (log α = +0.23) indicates children's general preference for same-ethnicity friends. To interpret the intercept, we calculate its antilogarithm and find that on average, children are 1.68 (α = antilog 0.23 = 1.68) times more likely to form same- than cross-ethnicity friendships. The main effect for individual ethnicity, showing more segregation among African Americans, is subsumed by the interaction with classroom majority. Figure 3.2 shows that African American students are much more likely to have segregated friendships in majority white (log α = +0.59, α = 3.88) than majority black classrooms (log α = +0.27, α = 1.88). European Americans were not substantially more segregated when they were a minority in majority black (log α = 0.18, α = 1.51) classrooms than when they were in the majority (log α = 0.07, α = 1.17).

Figure 3.2. Friendship Segregation by Child Ethnicity and Classroom Ethnic Composition

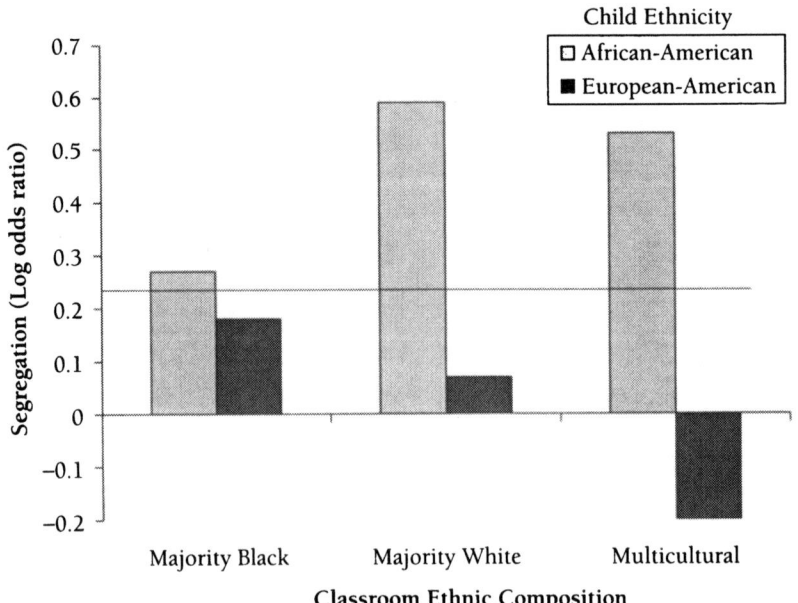

Peer Group Segregation. As shown in Table 3.4, significant effects in the model for peer group segregation are (1) the intercept (γ_{00} = +0.43), (2) the main effect of individual ethnicity (γ_{10} = +0.13), and (3) the interaction between individual ethnicity and classroom ethnic majority (γ_{11} = −0.16). The results for group affiliates are illustrated in Figure 3.3, which is read just like Figure 3.2. The horizontal line at γ_{00} = +0.43 is the grand mean, indicating preference among all children to affiliate in same-ethnicity groups (α = 2.69). African American children have more segregated peer groups than European American children, but this effect is qualified by the interaction with classroom majority. Figure 3.3 shows that African American children were more segregated (log α = +0.70, α = 5.01) than European American children (log α = +0.26, α = 1.82) in majority white classrooms. Figure 3.3 also suggests more segregation among African Americans (log α = +0.49, α = 3.09) than European Americans (log α = +0.25, α = 1.78) in multicultural classrooms, but this difference was not significant. In majority black classrooms, African American and European American children showed similar levels of peer group segregation (log αs = +0.39 and +0.50, respectively; αs = 2.45 and 3.16).

Likes-Most Segregation. As shown in Table 3.4, significant effects for likes-most segregation were (1) the intercept (γ_{00} = +0.35), (2) the main effect of individual ethnicity (γ_{10} = +0.11), and (3) the interaction of individual ethnicity and classroom ethnic majority (γ_{11} = −0.18). Figure 3.4

Figure 3.3. Peer Group (SCM) Segregation by Child Ethnicity and Classroom Ethnic Composition

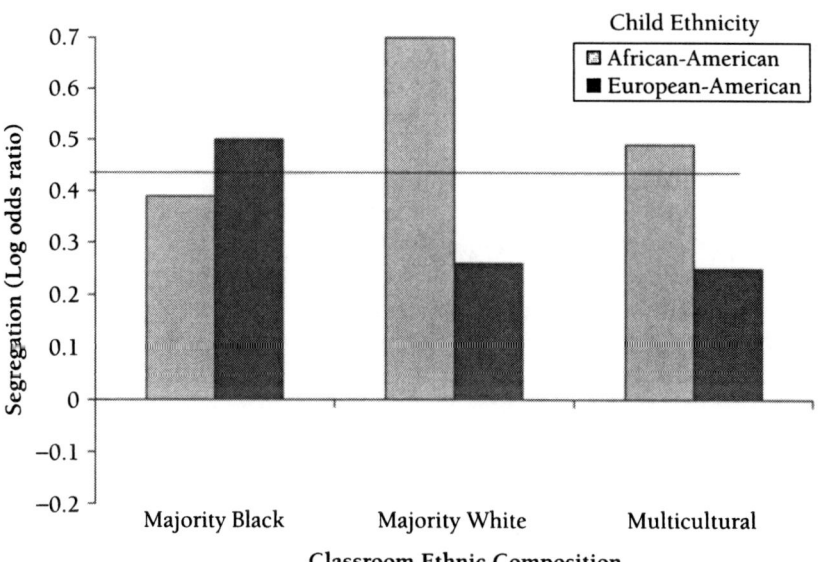

Figure 3.4. Likes-Most Segregation by Child Ethnicity and Classroom Ethnic Composition

```
Child Ethnicity
□ African-American
■ European-American
```

Y-axis: Segregation (Log odds ratio)
X-axis: Classroom Ethnic Composition — Majority Black, Majority White, Multicultural

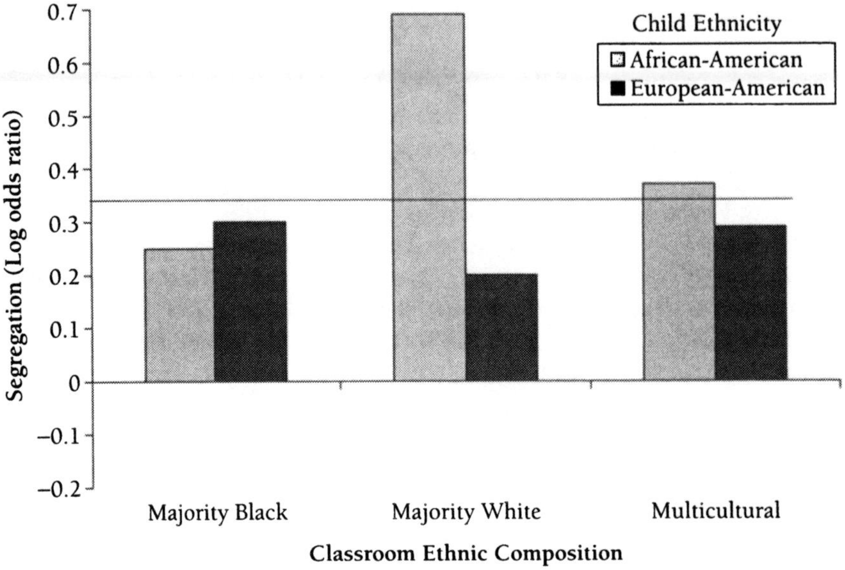

illustrates the interaction between individual ethnicity and classroom majority for segregated likes-most nominations.

Figure 3.4 shows that in majority white classrooms, the mutual likes-most nominations of African American children were largely same-ethnicity (log α = +0.70, α = 5.01) compared to European American children (log α = +0.20, α = 1.58). In contrast, segregation ratios were similar and modest for African American and European American children in classrooms that were majority black and multicultural.

Likes-Least Segregation. The multilevel model for antipathies in Table 3.4 shows three significant effects: (1) the intercept (γ_{00} = +0.14), (2) the main effect of classroom majority (γ_{01} = −0.16), and (3) the interaction of individual ethnicity and classroom ethnic majority (γ_{11} = +0.13). Overall, children were more likely to have cross-ethnicity than same-ethnicity antipathies (α = 1.38). The main effect of classroom majority shows that children form more cross-ethnic antipathies in majority white than majority black classrooms, but the effect varies by child ethnicity, as displayed in Figure 3.5. European Americans are much more likely to have cross-ethnic antipathies in majority white (log α = +0.47, α = 2.95) classrooms than they are in majority black (log α = −0.13, α = 0.74) classrooms. In comparison, African Americans had moderate levels of cross-ethnic antipathies across classroom contexts (log αs < +0.20).

Figure 3.5. Likes-Least Segregation by Child Ethnicity and Classroom Ethnic Composition

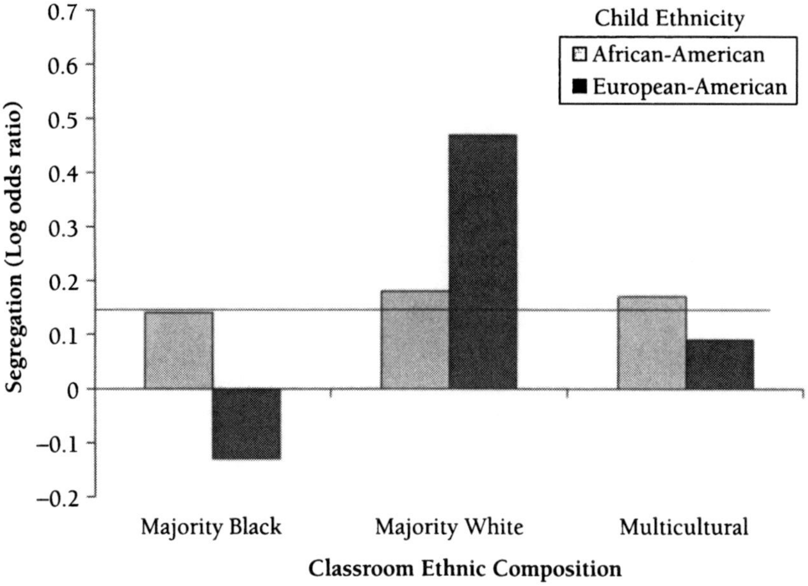

Discussion

Patterns of intergroup contact between third- and fourth-grade African American and European American children varied according to which ethnic group was the classroom majority. Unfortunately, we did not find substantial social integration in majority white classrooms (Brooks, 2007). African American children's positive ties were mostly with one another, and a high proportion of white children's antipathies were shared with black peers. African American segregation and European American antipathy may be complements (see Chapter Eight, this volume), reflecting linked developmental processes whose emergence should be tracked and changed. A culture of intergroup differentiation in majority white classrooms likely extends to social behavior. Rodkin, Farmer, Pearl, and Van Acker (2000) reported that African American children were equally likely to be popular across classroom contexts; however, black children's popularity was conjoined with aggression in mostly white classrooms, whereas in African American classrooms, popular black children were more likely to be viewed as prosocial (see also Jackson et al., 2006; Lease & Blake, 2005).

These relational patterns were specific to majority white classrooms. In majority black classrooms, African American and European American children had similar, moderate same-ethnic preferences. Multicultural classrooms did show segregation among African Americans on friendships and group affiliations, but without destructive cross-ethnic antipathies. We did not find clear benefits to diversity in multicultural classrooms, but there were significant limitations to this aspect of our analysis. We did not consider children who were neither European American nor African American. Our segregation indexes lost precision as fewer European American and African American children were included in its calculations. A more comprehensive sample is necessary to evaluate the benefits of diversity.

Other new directions could incorporate behavioral and status correlates of group placements, making use of newly developed social relations models (Card, Hodges, Little, & Hawley, 2005) and longitudinal, person-centered social network analyses. A still deeper understanding of interactional patterns will require gathering information through observation, interviews, and experiments, including information relevant to the development of implicit racial attitudes and ethnic identity, and residence.

The psychological significance of *Brown* v. *Board of Education* was the contention that it mattered to the developmental growth of black and white students as to whether they participated in integrated or segregated school environments (Rodkin, 1993). It still matters. Children's experiences in school have psychological significance when it comes to ethnic and race relations and other phenomena of personality and social development. Their intergroup (and interpersonal) relations are responsive to context and social construction and thus may require attention and intelligent oversight. Whatever the politics of the day, social network models of the development of children's intergroup relations have a dynamic contribution to make in building successful integrated schools.

References

Aboud, F. E., Mendelson, M. J., & Purdy, K. T. (2003). Cross-race peer relations and friendship quality. *International Journal of Behavioral Development, 27,* 165–173.

Asher, S. R., Parker, J. G., & Walker, D. L. (1996). Distinguishing friendships from acceptance: Implications for intervention and assessment. In W. M. Bukowski, A. F. Newcomb, & W. W. Hartup (Eds.), *The company they keep: Friendship in childhood and adolescence* (pp. 366–405). Cambridge: Cambridge University Press.

Bellmore, A. D., Witkow, M. R., Graham, S., & Juvonen, J. (2004). Beyond the individual: The impact of ethnic context and classroom behavioral norms on victims' adjustment. *Developmental Psychology, 40,* 1159–1172.

Brooks, D. (2007, July 6). The end of integration. *New York Times.* Retrieved July 7, 2007, from http://www.nytimes.com

Cairns, R. B., Xie, H., & Leung, M-C. (1998). The popularity of friendship and the neglect of social networks: Toward a new balance. In W. M. Bukowski & A. H. Cillessen (Eds.), *Sociometry then and now: Building on six decades of measuring children's experiences with the peer group* (pp. 25–53). San Francisco: Jossey-Bass.

Card, N. A., Hodges, E.V.E., Little, T. D., & Hawley, P. H. (2005). Gender effects in peer nominations for aggression and social status. *International Journal of Behavioral Development, 29,* 146–155.

Chang, L. (2004). The role of classroom norms in contextualizing the relations of children's social behaviors to peer acceptance. *Developmental Psychology, 40,* 691–702.
Clark, K. B., & Clark, M. P. (1947). Racial identification and preference in Negro children. In T. M. Newcomb & E. L. Hartley (Eds.), *Readings in social psychology* (pp. 169–178). New York: Holt.
Criswell, J. H. (1937). Racial cleavage in Negro-white groups. *Sociometry, 1,* 81–89.
Dubois, D. L., & Hirsch, B. J. (1990). School and neighborhood friendship patterns of blacks and whites in early adolescence. *Child Development, 61,* 524–536.
Gest, S. D., Graham-Bermann, S. A., & Hartup, W. W. (2001). Peer experience: Common and unique features of number of friendships, social network centrality, and sociometric status. *Social Development, 10,* 23–40.
Gorard, S., & Taylor, C. (2002). What is segregation? A comparison of measures in terms of "strong" and "weak" compositional invariance. *Sociology, 36,* 875–895.
Graham, S. (2007, March). *Peer relations, social problems, and social policy.* Panel presentation at the Peer Relationship Preconference at the Society for Research in Child Development, Boston.
Hallinan, M. T. (1982). Classroom racial composition and children's friendship. *Social Forces, 61,* 56–72.
Hamm, J. V., Brown, B. B., & Heck, D. J. (2005). Bridging the ethnic divide: Student and school characteristics in African American, Asian-descent, Latino, and white adolescents' cross-ethnic friend nominations. *Journal of Research on Adolescence, 15,* 21–46.
Hanish, L. D., & Guerra, N. G. (2000). The roles of ethnicity and school context in predicting children's victimization by peers. *American Journal of Community Psychology, 28,* 201–223.
Jackson, M. F., Barth, J. M., Powell, N., & Lochman, J. E. (2006). Classroom contextual effects of race on children's peer nominations. *Child Development, 77,* 1325–1337.
Juvonen, J., Nishina, A., & Graham, S. (2006). Ethnic diversity and perceptions of safety in urban middle schools. *Psychological Science, 17,* 393–400.
Kistner, J., Metzler, A., Gatlin, D., & Risi, S. (1993). Classroom racial proportions and children's peer relations: Race and gender effects. *Journal of Educational Psychology, 85,* 446–452.
Ladd, G. W. (2005). *Children's peer relations and social competence: A century of progress.* New Haven, CT: Yale University Press.
Lease, A. M., & Blake, J. J. (2005). A comparison of majority-race children with and without a minority-race friend. *Social Development, 14,* 20–41.
Moody, J. (2001). Race, school integration, and friendship segregation in America. *American Journal of Sociology, 107,* 679–716.
Moreno, J. L. (1934). *Who shall survive? A new approach to the problem of human interrelations.* Washington, DC: Nervous and Mental Disease Publishing.
Parents Involved in Community Schools v. Seattle School District, No. 1, 551 U.S._(2007).
Quillian, L., & Campbell, M. E. (2003). Beyond black and white: The present and future of multiracial friendship segregation. *American Sociological Review, 68,* 540–566.
Rodkin, P. C. (1993). The psychological reality of social constructions. *Ethnic and Racial Studies, 16,* 633–656.
Rodkin, P. C., Farmer, T. W., Pearl, R., & Van Acker, R. (2000). Heterogeneity of popular boys: Antisocial and prosocial configurations. *Developmental Psychology, 36,* 14–24.
Rodkin, P. C., Farmer, T. W., Pearl, R., & Van Acker, R. (2006). They're cool: Social status and group support for aggressive boys and girls. *Social Development, 15,* 175–204.
Rodkin, P. C., Pearl, R., Farmer, T. W., & Van Acker, R. (2003). Enemies in the gendered societies of middle childhood: Prevalence, stability, associations with social status, and aggression. In E.V.E. Hodges & N. Card (Eds.), *Enemies and the darker side of peer relationships* (pp. 73–88). San Francisco: Jossey-Bass.

Schofield, J. W., & Hausmann, L. R. (2004). School desegregation and social science research. *American Psychologist, 59,* 538–546.

Singleton, L. C., & Asher, S. R. (1979). Racial integration and children's peer preferences: An investigation of developmental and cohort differences. *Child Development, 50,* 936–941.

Tajfel, H. (1970). Experiments in intergroup discrimination. *Scientific American, 223,* 96–102.

Tseng, V., & Seidman, E. (2007). A systems framework for understanding social settings. *American Journal of Community Psychology, 39,* 217–228.

U.S. Commission on Civil Rights. (2006, October). *The benefits of racial and ethnic diversity in elementary and secondary education.* Retrieved May 2, 2007, from http://www.usccr.gov.

Williams, J. (2007, June 29). Don't mourn *Brown v. Board of Education. New York Times.* Retrieved July 7, 2007, from http://www.nytimes.com.

PHILIP C. RODKIN *is an associate professor of child development in the Departments of Educational Psychology and Psychology at the University of Illinois at Urbana-Champaign.*

TRAVIS WILSON *is a doctoral candidate in the Department of Educational Psychology at the University of Illinois at Urbana-Champaign.*

HAI-JEONG AHN *is a doctoral candidate in the Department of Educational Psychology at the University of Illinois at Urbana-Champaign.*

Girls and boys were more similar than different in the structural features of their social groups and networks in early adolescence. Boys' groups were somewhat larger than girls' groups, but contrary to prominent theoretical views, there were no systematic sex differences in tight-knittedness or in the salience of status hierarchies.

4

Features of Groups and Status Hierarchies in Girls' and Boys' Early Adolescent Peer Networks

Scott D. Gest, Alice J. Davidson, Kelly L. Rulison, James Moody, Janet A. Welsh

The near universality of gender segregation in middle childhood and early adolescence has stimulated extensive research on sex differences in peer relationship processes (Leaper, 1994; Maccoby, 1990, 1998; Underwood, 2004). Maccoby (1990, 1998), for example, makes the case for the existence of substantial sex differences in children's peer group structures and norms, discourse and relational styles, activity preferences, and values and expectations for relationships; and she argues that children's development within these two distinct gender cultures may strengthen harmful and limiting gender stereotypes. Recent reviews of the literature suggest that although some claims of two-cultures theory have clear empirical support, such as strong preference for same-sex peers over other-sex peers (Fabes, Martin, & Hanish, 2003), others receive mixed or limited support (Rose & Rudolph, 2006; Underwood, 2004). In particular, claims about sex differences in children's peer relations have frequently been made without attending to the peer group structures in which those differences occur. For example, of the 215 studies of sex differences in peer relations that Rose and Rudolph (2006) reviewed, only 16 studies quantified sex differences in the larger organizational patterns of same-sex relationships (examples are dyadic versus group interaction patterns, group size, and network dominance hierarchies). The goal of this study is to begin to fill this gap by

applying concepts and measures from social network analysis to test theory-driven hypotheses regarding two enduring questions about similarities and differences in girls' and boys' peer networks.

The first question concerns features related to group strength: Are girls' and boys' networks equally likely to be organized into sets of groups that are internally tightly knit yet distinct from one another? A tightly knit group of friends, for example, is one in which friendships exist between most pairs of individuals within the group (high density), most friendship nominations from one person to another are reciprocated (high reciprocity), and most pairs of individuals who share a common friend are also friends with each other (high transitivity; Scott, 2000). Distinctiveness, in contrast, refers to the degree to which individuals direct their social ties to members of their group rather than to individuals in other groups. The second question concerns status hierarchies: Are girls' and boys' networks and groups similarly characterized by an unequal distribution of status? In this case, status is an individual-level concept (for example, receiving many friendship or liking nominations; Borgatti, 2005; Freeman, 1979), and centralization is a group- or network-level concept describing the degree to which status is concentrated in one or a few individuals (Wasserman & Faust, 1994).

Two-Cultures Theory and Boys' and Girls' Peer Network Structures

Maccoby (1990, 1998; Maccoby & Jacklin, 1974) has suggested that because girls and boys interact mostly within same-sex peer groups in middle childhood and preadolescence, they develop in two distinct gendered cultures. Within these two cultures, boys' and girls' peer groups can be contrasted on several broad dimensions: play styles and activity preferences, discourse, friendships, and group strength and power. From this perspective, differences in boys' and girls' cultures have important developmental consequences, including the strengthening of harmful and limiting gender stereotypes (Leaper, 1994) and the development of conflicting goals and values (Maccoby, 1998), which may hinder successful other-gender interactions.

Despite limited empirical research on some of these issues (Rose & Rudolph, 2006), two-cultures theorists conclude that girls are more dyad oriented and less group oriented than are boys, resulting in smaller and less differentiated group structures among girls, and that girls' interactions are characterized by more intimacy, more cooperation, and less competition, resulting in less salient status hierarchies (Maccoby & Jacklin, 1974; Maccoby, 1990; 1998). Here, we briefly review findings from four distinct research traditions on the issues of group tight-knittedness, distinctiveness, and status hierarchies. In general, the existing empirical literature does not support strong claims of gender differences in peer network structures (Thorne, 1993; Underwood, 2004). Instead, seemingly contradictory findings regarding sex differences likely reflect methodological differences in work arising from distinct research traditions.

Observational Studies of Peer Interactions in Naturalistic Settings. One important research tradition is the quantitative coding and analysis of children's interactions in natural settings or naturally occurring situations. Research in this tradition includes observations of young children in preschool settings (Fabes et al., 2003), field experiments in which researchers observe intragroup behavior among children who are randomly assigned to cabins with same-sex peers (Parker & Seal, 1996; Omark & Edelman, 1975; Savin-Williams, 1979, 1980), and observations of adolescents in school and community settings (Coleman, 1961; Dunphy, 1963). Evidence from these studies generally supports the conclusion that boys form more tightly knit and distinctive group structures. For example, preschool boys were more likely than girls to play in same-sex groups, whereas girls were more likely than boys to play in same-sex dyads during free play (Fabes et al., 2003). In studies of nine- to fifteen-year-old youth in camp settings, boys were more oriented toward their own group than were girls (Savin-Williams, 1979, 1980), and the density of friendship ties within cabins increased over time for boys but decreased over time for girls (Parker & Seal, 1996). Finally, adolescent boys aggregated in large groups of around ten youth, whereas girls virtually never did so and were most often observed in dyads (Coleman, 1961; Dunphy, 1963).

These same studies are in less agreement regarding the existence of sex differences in status hierarchies. For example, Savin-Williams (1979, 1980) found that males formed more reliable and pronounced dominance status hierarchies (see also Omark & Edelman, 1975). In contrast, Coleman's study (1961) indicated that girls expressed more consensus than boys regarding the identity of the highest-status same-sex group at their school, suggesting that status hierarchies were perhaps more salient among girls than among boys.

Studies of Peer Interactions in Experimenter-Controlled Settings. One limitation of quantitative observations in naturalistic settings is that observed sex differences may be artifacts of differences in the activity contexts that girls and boys choose rather than reflecting more fundamental sex differences in the nature of peer network dynamics (Underwood, 2004). Observing peer interactions in controlled play contexts circumvents this limitation and suggests emerging sex differences in group orientation. In play groups of four to six year olds, for example, girls' dyadic interactions were fewer in number but longer in duration than those of boys, but among six year olds, boys were more likely to spend time in group-level interactions (Benenson, Apostoleris, & Parnass, 1997). Evidence from other studies suggests that status hierarchies may be more salient within small groups of girls. In one study of groups of four- and five-year-old children, groups of four same-sex children were presented with a movie-viewer apparatus that required cooperation from two group members in order for a third member to see the movie, with no designated role for the fourth member (Charlesworth & Dzur, 1987). Results indicated that time spent viewing the movie, engaging in one of the two cooperative roles, or as the bystander were less equally distributed within girls' groups, suggesting that status hierarchies were more prominent among girls. Similarly, Smith and Inder (1993) observed that bids for social entry were more likely to be rejected in play groups of three- to five-year-old girls. Overall, these experimenter-controlled play group studies support the emergence of a greater group orientation among boys, but they do not support the notion that status hierarchies are less relevant for girls.

Ethnographic Studies of Peer Networks and Groups. To better capture the richness of peer network dynamics, several researchers have conducted detailed ethnographic studies of preadolescent peer networks (Adler & Adler, 1996; Goodwin, 2002; Merten, 2005; Thorne, 1993). These studies differ from the observational studies described above in that the researchers actively participated in the social settings they were seeking to understand by conducting interviews and collecting qualitative data on naturally occurring conversations among participants. These ethnographic studies, which have focused primarily on status hierarchies and group dynamics, are strikingly consistent in describing the equal salience of status hierarchies within girls' and boys' peer networks. For example, in a study of third to sixth graders, Adler and Adler (1996) described four prominent status levels among both girls and boys (populars, wannabes, middle group and social isolates) and found that girls' and boys' networks were comparably characterized by competition and cooperation, inclusion and exclusion (Adler, Kless, & Adler, 1992). Similarly, Goodwin (2002) observed complex language and social interactive practices involved with social exclusion and ridicule at lunch and recess among ten- to twelve-year-old girls. Merten (1995, 2005) described seventh- and eighth-grade girls' use of "meanness" and social exclusion to distinguish themselves as groups within the larger social network and to contest positions of status hierarchy within their own groups, and Thorne (1993) concluded that status hierarchies were equally salient among girls and boys despite clear sex differences in the basis of these hierarchies (for example, sports were more salient for boys). Overall, these ethnographic studies are consistent in pointing out the equal salience of status hierarchies for girls and boys.

Sociometric Studies of Friendship and "Hanging Around Together." A fourth research tradition is based on the patterning of youths' friendship nominations and multi-informant peer reports of which classmates "hang around together a lot." Eder and Hallinan's longitudinal study (1978) of transitivity in the friendships of fifth and sixth graders is particularly relevant. They found that girls had more exclusive dyadic friendships than boys did. In addition, over the course of the school year, girls' dyadic friendships tended to remain exclusive, whereas boys' expanded to include a third member, suggesting that boys were more oriented toward group affiliations than were girls. Sex differences in the salience of group structures identified from friendship or "hang around together" nominations (Cairns, Cairns, Neckerman, Gest, & Gariepy, 1988) have not been widely reported, however, suggesting that any difference in group orientation may be relatively modest. Furthermore, few studies report sex differences in the predictive validity of measures of liking and disliking (Parker & Asher, 1987), suggesting that status hierarchies are equally salient among girls and boys, at least at the level of the whole-classroom network.

Summary. In sum, studies from these four distinct research traditions have produced mixed results. With regard to group orientation and features of group strength, observational and experimental play group studies support the conclusion that boys form larger, more distinct, and tightly knit group structures, with more mixed support coming from sociometric studies. With regard to status hierarchies, however, observational studies have produced contradictory results, experimental play group studies suggest stronger status hierarchies among girls, and ethnographic and sociometric studies do not suggest any sex differences.

The Study: Group Features and Status Hierarchies

Existing research is limited and difficult to integrate because researchers have not always clearly distinguished between different levels of analysis (network versus group), different types of social ties (observable interactions versus affective ties), and different developmental periods (childhood versus adolescence). In our study, we operate from a sociometric research tradition and attend to each of these distinctions. We begin by identifying same-sex networks (classrooms or grade-cohorts) and groups (subsets of classmates who hang around together). At each of these levels of analysis, we consider both interaction-based ties (hanging around together) and affect-based ties (friendship and liking). At each level, we examine tight-knittedness in terms of the density, reciprocity and transitivity of ties, and we measure status hierarchies in terms of the centralization of status indicators. The distinctiveness of groups can be examined only at the level of networks, which contain multiple groups. By adopting a longitudinal design from fifth to seventh grades, we focus on early adolescents before and after their transition to middle school in sixth grade, a developmental period characterized by strong preference for affiliation with same-sex peers.

Regarding group orientation and tight-knittedness, discrepant findings in the studies reviewed above may reflect important differences in measurement strategy (Underwood, 2004). Studies relying on direct observation consistently detect a stronger orientation toward larger and more tightly knit groups among boys, but these differences appear to be less salient when ties are measured in terms of more generalized patterns of affiliation captured by sociometric studies of hanging around, friendship, and liking. Because we adopted the latter methods, we did not expect to find sex differences in the tight-knittedness of girls' and boys' networks or groups. With regard to status hierarchies, the mixed evidence did not support a strong directional hypothesis: two camp studies found stronger hierarchies among boys, but studies of contrived play groups suggest more pronounced hierarchies among girls, and ethnographies and sociometric studies suggest that status hierarchies are equally salient for girls and boys.

Methods

We report results from a five-year longitudinal study of friendships and social groups among early adolescents.

Participants. Participants were 427 youth (193 girls, 234 boys) enrolled in three consecutive grade cohorts of a public school in a small working-class community in the northeastern United States (for details, see Gest, Rulison, Davidson, & Welsh, in press). For this study, we report data from the fall and spring assessments in fifth and seventh grades. Participation rates exceeded 90 percent at each assessment because relatively few students moved away and students new to the school were recruited in the fall each year. Almost all students at the school (99 percent) were Caucasian, reflecting the demographics of the larger community served by the school district.

Measures of Networks and Groups. Networks and groups were identified on the basis of student reports obtained during group-administered surveys.

Multi-Informant Groups. We constructed multi-informant groups using Cairns's social cognitive map (SCM) method. Seventh-grade students were asked, "Are there some kids in your grade who hang around together a lot? List the names of the kids in each of the different groups in your grade. Try to think of as many groups as you can." Fifth-grade students were asked the same question with respect to students in their classroom. Space was provided for students to list up to nine groups with up to ten individuals per group, and they were free to list themselves in a group. Prior studies document that the frequency of being named to the same group is correlated with observable interaction rates ($r = .56$; Cairns, Perrin, & Cairns, 1985; Gest, Farmer, Cairns, & Xie, 2003). Networks refer to the whole classroom (in fifth grade) or grade (in seventh grade) in which students were embedded. Nominations for each network were organized into a symmetric co-nomination matrix in which off-diagonal cells indicated the total number of times two individuals were named to the same group. Values along the diagonal indicated the number of times a given child was named to any social group.

We applied principal component analysis to identify the groups within each network. Briefly, we extracted all components with eigenvalues greater than 1.0 that, after varimax rotation, were defined by at least three individuals whose primary loading was on that component (for details, see Gest, Moody, & Rulison, 2007). This procedure allows the possibility of membership in more than one group, but for the analyses here, we consider only each student's primary group membership. We present results separately for network-level and group-level analyses. For network-level analyses, there were eighteen networks each for girls and boys in fifth grade (six classroom networks for each of the three grade cohorts) and three networks each for girls and boys in seventh grade (one grade network for each of the three grade cohorts). For group-level analyses, we identified ninety-one (fall) and eighty-nine (spring) groups in fifth grade and eighty-four (fall) and seventy-nine (spring) groups in seventh grade. Given our focus on sex differences, we exclude from our analyses the 18 percent of fifth-grade groups and 27 percent of seventh-grade groups that were mixed gender. This resulted in seventy-six (fall) and seventy-one (spring) groups in fifth grade, and fifty-nine groups in both fall and spring of seventh grade.

Self-Reported Friendships and Liking. Students were asked to list the names of their friends in their classroom (fifth grade) or grade (seventh grade). Space was provided for students to list up to ten names. In a subsequent portion of the survey, students identified peers who met each of twelve descriptors. For the analyses here, we focus on responses to the prompt, "Who are the kids in your classroom/grade you like the most?" Space was provided for up to six names.

Measures of Tight-Knittedness, Distinctiveness, and Status Hierarchies. All network indexes were computed with Statistical Analysis Software (SAS) routines developed by Moody (2000). The sociograms illustrating each index were created with the cross-platform R program using the network library (Handcock, Hunter, Goodreau, Butts, & Morris, 2003). All indexes of tight-knittedness, distinctiveness, and status hierarchy were computed separately for friendship ties and for "liked-most" ties.

Tight-Knittedness. We characterize the tight-knittedness of networks and groups with three indexes that have been used in prior developmental research (Hallinan, 1980; Parker & Seal, 1996). *Density* is the average value of ties taken over all possible dyads (possible range from 0 to 1). Low-density networks have relatively few or primarily unidirectional ties among members, whereas high-density networks have relatively many and primarily bidirectional ties. *Reciprocity* is a simple dyadic index of the proportion of all nominations that are reciprocated. Finally, *transitivity* is defined as the proportion of all potentially closed triads that are actually closed. It is calculated as the proportion of all two-step paths ($i \to j, j \to k$) that are also direct paths ($i \to k$).

Distinctiveness. The distinctiveness of groups within a network is not typically quantified in developmental research despite the relevance of this concept for discussions of group orientation (Rose & Rudolph, 2006). Distinctiveness refers to how often social ties fall within rather than between groups, and one intuitive index is relative density, defined as the density of ties falling within groups divided by the density of ties that fall outside groups. As a second index, we use Freeman's network segregation index (1972), which is calculated as the difference between the number of observed cross-group ties and the number of randomly expected cross-group ties, divided by the number of randomly expected cross-group ties. The value is 0 when ties are distributed randomly across groups and reaches 1.0 when all ties fall within separate groups.

Status Hierarchy. For any given index of individual status within the network or group, the strength of the status hierarchy can be measured in terms of centralization, or the extent to which status is concentrated in one or a few individuals. Calculating the variance of individual status scores within a group or network gets at the same phenomenon, but centralization indexes are preferred due to technical challenges in scaling variance scores across networks (Wasserman & Faust, 1994). In this, we measure individual status in terms of the number of times individuals are named as "liked most" or as friends, but we adjust these scores to account for the status of the individuals who provide those nominations. This is the notion behind indexes of power centrality developed by Bonacich (1987): for individuals who receive the same number of nominations, power centrality varies according to the status of the individuals who "sent" those nominations (that is, power centrality is higher if an individual receives nominations from high-status peers).

The ranges of tight-knittedness, group distinctiveness, and status hierarchy observed in the study are illustrated in Figure 4.1. For each index, low groups or networks fall approximately one standard deviation below the sample average, and high groups or networks fall approximately one standard deviation above the sample average. For density, the low group lacks many potential ties within the group, whereas the high group contains nearly all possible ties. For relative density, the two SCM-based groups in the low network are difficult to discern because friendship nominations are nearly as likely to occur between as within groups, whereas in the high network, nearly all friendship nominations occur within the two SCM groups. For centralization, all individuals in the low group receive nearly the same number of friendship nominations, whereas individuals in the high group vary more widely in the number of received nominations.

Results

We begin by examining network-level tight-knittedness, group distinctiveness, and status hierarchies; then we describe these features at the group level.

Network-Level Analyses. In fifth grade, there were eighteen networks each for girls and boys (six classroom networks for each of the three grade-cohorts), so tests of sex differences were conducted with a $2 \times 2 \times 2$ ANOVA, with sex as a between-subjects factor and social tie (friendship versus liking) and season (fall versus spring) as within-subject factors. Here, we focus only on main effects or interactions testing sex differences and include estimates of effect size (d). We present results for each of the three grade-level networks for seventh-grade girls and boys at a descriptive level.

Tight-Knittedness of Networks. Among fifth graders, there were no reliable sex differences in the density, reciprocity, or transitivity of friendship

Figure 4.1. Patterns of Directional Friendship Ties Within a Group (Density, Centralization) or Same-Sex Classroom Network (Relative Density)

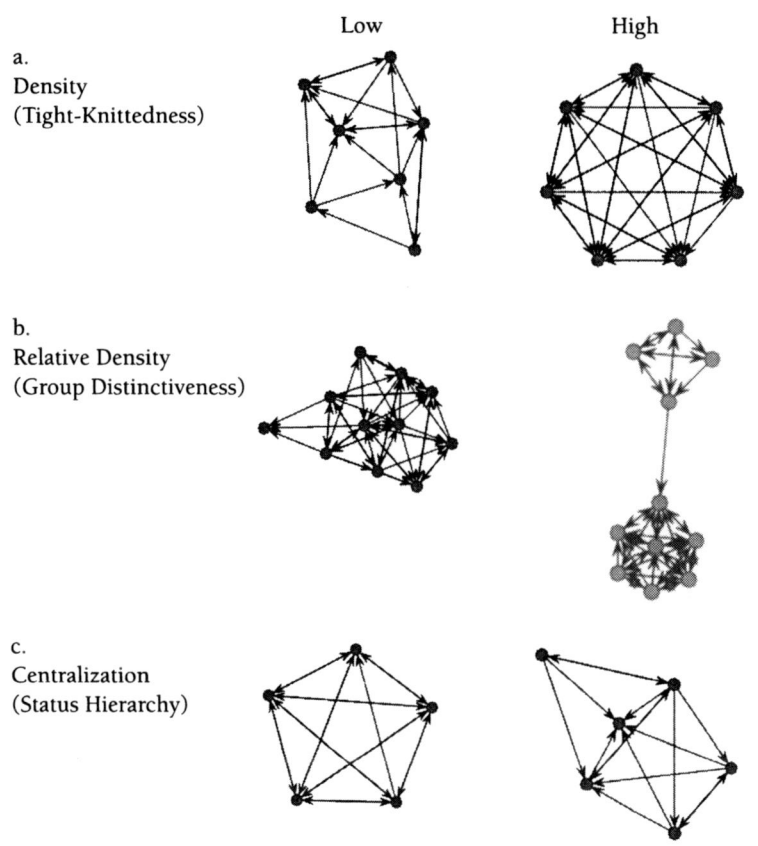

a. Density (Tight-Knittedness)

b. Relative Density (Group Distinctiveness)

c. Centralization (Status Hierarchy)

or liking ties within same-sex peer networks. For density, sex differences did not approach significance, $F(1,34) = .16$, NS, and were very small in magnitude ($d_{friend} = .01$, $d_{liking} = .26$; positive values of d indicate higher scores for girls). Overall, youth had friendship ties with roughly 48 percent of their same-sex classmates and had "liked most" ties with 29 percent of their same-sex classmates (see Table 4.1, top two rows). The reciprocity of social ties did not differ reliably by sex, $F(1,34) = 2.27$, $p = .14$, but observed reciprocity tended to be modestly higher for boys ($d_{friend} = -.36$, $d_{liking} = -.38$). Overall, 53 percent of friendship nominations and 40 percent of liking nominations were reciprocated. There was no indication of sex differences in the transitivity of friendship or liking nominations, $F(1,34) = .003$, ns ($d_{friend} = .04$, $d_{liking} = -.06$): overall, 64 percent of friendship ties and

Table 4.1. Same-Sex Peer Networks in Fifth Grade: Tight-Knittedness, Distinctiveness, and Status Hierarchies

	Fall		Spring		
	Girls	Boys	Girls	Boys	F(sex)
Tight-Knittedness					
Density					
Friendship	.49 (.12)	.48 (.14)	.46 (.11)	.47 (.11)	.16 NS
Liked most	.29 (.11)	.27 (.10)	.32 (.10)	.29 (.08)	
Reciprocity					
Friendship	.48 (.17)	.55 (.15)	.53 (.14)	.56 (.13)	2.27
Liked most	.37 (.15)	.42 (.12)	.38 (.12)	.42 (.13)	p = .14
Transitivity					
Friendship	.62 (.12)	.64 (.11)	.66 (.12)	.63 (.11)	.003 NS
Liked most	.46 (.21)	.53 (.13)	.58 (.11)	.54 (.15)	
Distinctiveness					
Freeman segregation					
Friendship	.17 (.17)	.28 (.25)	.20 (.16)	.27 (.23)	1.71 NS
Liked most	.40 (.23)	.44 (.31)	.37 (.23)	.50 (.23)	
Relative density					
Friendship	2.79 (1.10)	3.25 (3.10)	3.22 (2.79)	3.92 (3.69)	.58 NS
Liked most	5.56 (3.08)	6.09 (6.23)	6.30 (5.89)	8.20 (8.27)	
Status hierarchy					
BP centralization					
Friendship	.53 (.15)	.58 (.22)	.57 (.21)	.52 (.21)	.13 NS
Liked most	.34 (.11)	.39 (.20)	.43 (.13)	.43 (.15)	

53 percent of liking ties evidenced transitivity. There was no clear pattern of sex differences in these indexes in the small number of seventh-grade networks, but the density, reciprocity, and transitivity of ties in these larger networks clearly declined dramatically from fifth to seventh grades: for friendship ties, density declined from .48 to .11, reciprocity declined from .53 to .32, and transitivity declined from .53 to .31.

Distinctiveness. Among fifth graders, there were no reliable sex differences in the distinctiveness of groups within same-sex classroom networks. For the Freeman segregation index, observed values suggested modestly greater distinctiveness in boys' groups (d_{friend} = −.42, d_{liking} = −.36), but these differences were not statistically reliable, $F(1,32) = 1.71$, $p = .17$. Differences in the relative density of ties within and between groups were even smaller (d_{friend} = −.20, d_{liking} = −.18), $F(1,32) = .58$, NS. Overall, friendship ties were three to four times denser, and liked-most ties were five to eight times denser within groups than between groups. No clear sex differences emerged in seventh grade, but the distinctiveness of groups was higher in seventh grade: for example, the relative density of friendship increased from three to four in fifth grade to around ten in seventh grade.

Status Hierarchies. Among fifth graders, there was no indication of sex differences in the degree to which status was centralized in a small number of individuals, $F(1,34) = .13$, ns, ($d_{friend} = -.01$, $d_{liking} = -.12$), although centralization of status was notably higher for friendship ties than for liking ties. In contrast, among seventh graders, a clear sex difference emerged: for all three networks, the centralization of friendship nominations was much higher for boys in both the fall and spring. There were much smaller and less consistent sex differences in the centralization of nominations as liked most.

Group-Level Analyses. Because each network described above was composed of multiple groups, we were able to conduct parametric tests of sex differences at both grade levels. However, because the composition of groups changed from fall to spring, groups (unlike classrooms) could not be treated as a within-subjects factor. Consequently, we conducted separate 2 × 2 × 2 ANOVAs for the fall and spring assessments, with sex and grade as between-subjects factors and social tie (friendship versus liking) as a within-subjects factor. As with the network-level analyses, we focus on main or interaction effects testing for sex differences (see Table 4.2).

Group Size. In the fall, for fifth and seventh graders, girls' groups were significantly smaller than boys' groups, $F(1,131) = 7.82$, $p < .01$, with the means indicating that girls' groups had roughly one fewer person than boys' groups ($d = -.49$). In the spring, sex differences in group size were somewhat smaller ($d = -.35$) and were no longer reliable, $F(1,126) = 2.65$, $p = .11$. In both fall and spring, groups were reliably larger in seventh grade.

Tight-Knittedness of Groups. In the fall, the density of friendship and liking ties was greater within girls' groups than within boys' groups, $F(1,127) = 5.97$, $p < .05$ ($d_{friend} = .37$, $d_{liking} = .45$). Figure 4.2 displays the sex difference for friendship in the density of nominations between groups. Note here the prominence of within-gender variability relative to the modest between-gender differences. By the spring assessments, however, sex differences in density of ties had diminished and were no longer reliable, $F(1,124) = .14$, ns ($d_{friend} = -.06$, $d_{liking} = .20$).

A similar but weaker pattern existed for reciprocity: sex differences favoring girls approached reliability in the fall, $F(1,126) = 2.84$, $p < .10$, but not in the spring, $F(1,121) = .06$, NS. There were no reliable sex differences in the transitivity of ties within groups at either assessment, fall $F(1,126) = .01$ NS, spring $F(1,121) = 1.35$ NS. (The grade-by-gender interaction term suggested by the means in Table 4.2 did not approach statistical significance.)

Status Hierarchies. There were no sex differences in the degree to which friendship or liking nominations were centralized in a small number of individuals: fall, $F(1,126) = .16$, NS; spring, $F(1,116) = .27$, NS. In both fall and spring, a significant tie by grade interaction reflected the fact that the centralization of friendship nominations (but not liking nominations) increased between fifth and seventh grade for girls and boys.

Table 4.2. "Hang Around Together" Groups: Size, Tight-Knittedness, and Status Hierarchies

	Fall			Spring		
	Girls	Boys	F(sex)	Girls	Boys	F(sex)
Group size						
Fifth grade	4.97 (1.75)	6.03 (1.79)	7.82**	4.61 (1.53)	5.67 (1.65)	2.65
Seventh grade	6.00 (2.41)	7.29 (3.34)		6.76 (2.96)	7.18 (3.65)	p = .11
Tight-knittedness						
Density						
Fifth grade						
Friendship	.72 (.22)	.67 (.14)		.71 (.21)	.71 (.16)	
Like most	.51 (.19)	.43 (.21)		.57 (.17)	.51 (.17)	
Seventh Grade			5.97*			.14 NS
Friendship	.55 (.20)	.44 (.23)		.45 (.18)	.48 (.26)	
Like most	.38 (.23)	.29 (.16)		.31 (.21)	.29 (.16)	
Reciprocity						
Fifth grade						
Friendship	.70 (.28)	.60 (.22)		.64 (.34)	.67 (.20)	
Like most	.48 (.31)	.49 (.29)		.51 (.34)	.56 (.27)	
Seventh grade			2.84+			.06 NS
Friendship	.54 (.23)	.47 (.29)		.48 (.27)	.49 (.27)	
Like most	.44 (.29)	.32 (.25)		.41 (.33)	.34 (.25)	
Transitivity						
Fifth grade						
Friendship	.78 (.23)	.74 (.21)		.79 (.28)	.74 (.24)	
Like most	.56 (.35)	.48 (.32)		.67 (.25)	.55 (.28)	
Seventh grade			.01 NS			1.35 NS
Friendship	.54 (.31)	.53 (.24)		.59 (.24)	.56 (.26)	
Like most	.38 (.37)	.48 (.32)		.50 (.29)	.48 (.30)	
Status hierarchy						
BP centralization						
Fifth grade						
Friendship	.46 (.33)	.53 (.25)		.43 (.34)	.44 (.28)	
Like most	.59 (.29)	.64 (.25)		.56 (.26)	.61 (.23)	
Seventh grade			.16 NS			.27 NS
Friendship	.55 (.26)	.54 (.24)		.56 (.25)	.54 (.24)	
Like most	.56 (.25)	.50 (.24)		.48 (.24)	.50 (.28)	

$**p < .01$. $*p < .05$. $+p < .10$.

Discussion

Our findings suggest that girls and boys are more similar than different in the structural features of their social groups and networks. Across the four early adolescence assessments, girls and boys were similar in their tendency to form same-sex peer groups that were distinct, tightly knit, and charac-

Figure 4.2. Sex Differences in the Density of Friendship Nomination Within Groups

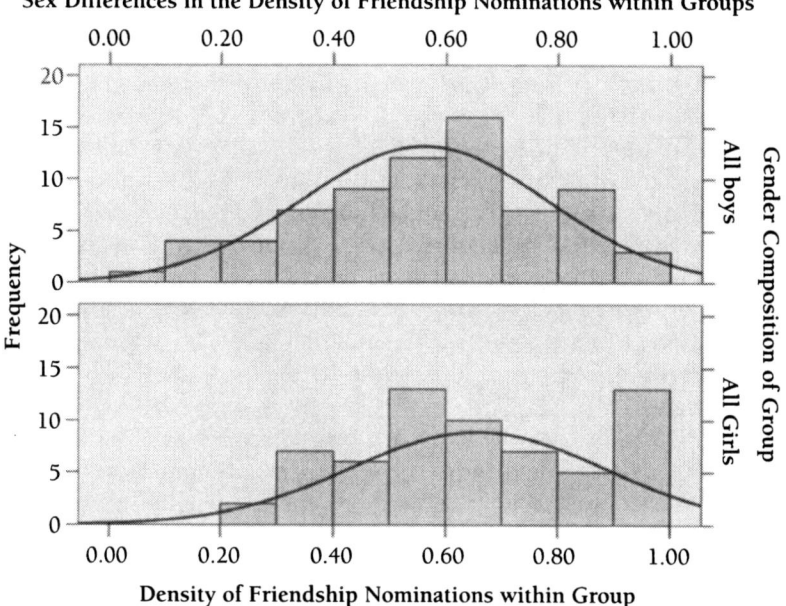

terized by status hierarchies. The sex differences that we identified were small in magnitude, limited to particular indexes or developmental periods, and in some instances ran counter to prior research. Put differently, within-sex variability was more pronounced than between-sex differences. In contrast to well-documented sex differences in the interactive styles within same-sex groups in childhood and early adolescence (Maccoby, 1990, 1998), the findings suggest that strong claims about sex differences in structural features of same-sex social groups and networks in early adolescence are not justified.

Two-cultures theorists (Maccoby, 1990) assert that boys are more group oriented than girls, with the consequence that boys' groups are larger, more distinct from one another, and more tightly knit. We found limited support for this perspective even though the number of groups we considered ($N = 265$) was large compared to other studies that have been the basis for conclusions about sex differences in peer group structures (Rose & Rudolph, 2006). On the one hand, girls' groups were consistently smaller than boys' groups, and there was a statistically unreliable trend for boys (more than girls) to direct their friendship and liking nominations within (rather than between) groups. On the other hand, girls' groups had, on average, only about one fewer person than boys' groups, differences in group distinctiveness were even smaller and unreliable, and there were no sex differences in the reciprocity or transitivity of within-group ties. Moreover, in the fall, girls' groups were actually denser than boys' groups in terms of patterns of liking and friendship nominations. Overall, these patterns support the conclusion that although girls' groups may be somewhat smaller than boys' groups, girls and boys are equally group oriented and form similarly tightly knit groups.

We also found limited support for the view that status hierarchies are more salient in boys' networks and groups. In all three seventh-grade networks, the centralization of friendship nominations was notably higher among boys than among girls, indicating a greater tendency for a relatively small number of boys to receive many nominations. However, this difference did not extend to liking nominations, group-level differences in seventh grade, or any of the measures of status centralization in fifth grade. These findings are consistent with those of ethnographic studies (Adler & Adler, 1995; Goodwin, 2002; Merten, 1995, 2005; Thorne, 1993) and other research suggesting that status hierarchies exist to a similar degree for girls and boys (Charlesworth & Dzur, 1987; Smith & Inder, 1993). However, it may be important to use multiple indexes of status to explore potential developmental changes in the salience of status hierarchies and explore potential sex differences in the determinants of status hierarchies (Goodwin, 2002) or the peer acceptance of high-status individuals (Sebanc, Pearce, Cheatham, & Gunnar, 2003).

Two types of integrative studies will be especially important in future studies of girls' and boys' peer networks and groups. First, there is a need to map processes occurring within single settings and across relatively brief time frames (seconds, minutes) onto processes that operate across multiple settings and more extended time spans (weeks, months). For example, studies revealing sex differences in group orientation often use direct observations in specific interaction settings or over relatively short periods of time (Benenson, 1990, 1993; Fabes et al., 2003), whereas we found few sex differences in similar indexes when we abstracted group structures from peer reports that required respondents to distill information across a range of settings (for example, classrooms, playgrounds) over an extended period of time. Studies that include multiple contexts and time frames will be critical in clarifying how the well-documented sex differences in interactive styles within girls' and boys' groups (Maccoby, 1990, 1998) could lead to similar peer group and network structures over longer time frames.

Second, there is a need to integrate studies of the structural features of groups and networks with studies of the discourse practices and behaviors taking place within them. Group and network structures presumably emerge in part from discourse patterns among peers, yet these ways of communicating do not exist outside a relational (dyad, group, network) context. Existing research tends to focus on one process or the other, with ethnographic work focusing on language, conversation, and discourse practices (Goodwin,

2002) and sociometric studies focusing on structural patterns (Eder & Hallinan, 1978). By simultaneously examining children's discourse practices, their behaviors, and their peer group structure (Leaper & Smith, 2004), researchers can pose important new questions about peer group dynamics. For example, do networks or groups characterized by pronounced status hierarchies and low levels of reciprocity or transitivity foster more bully-victim interactions? Does a shift toward more cooperative and less competitive discourse patterns produce more transitive ties and a weaker status hierarchy? Do these processes work similarly for girls and boys or contribute to gender differences in behavior?

Two developmental trends suggested by the results we present are also worthy of further study. First, some sex differences varied within the school year (for example, group density) or across grade levels (for example, network friendship centralization), suggesting it is important to consider how sex differences may emerge within school years or across longer intervals, perhaps in the context of changing school structures (for example, transition to middle school). Second, as mixed-sex groups become increasingly common in early adolescence, it is important to clarify whether these groups share the characteristics of same-sex groups or whether they have unique features. In either case, two-cultures theorists (Maccoby, 1990; Maccoby, 1998) suggest that it is during this developmental period when the dramatically different interactive styles of same-sex peer groups in childhood begin to play out in a less sex-segregated social world.

Overall, these findings suggest that girls and boys are more alike than different in terms of the structural features of their same-sex peer groups and networks in early adolescence. As with other studies of sex differences (Maccoby & Jacklin, 1974), differences between boys and girls were relatively small compared to within-sex variability. In this regard, the notable within-sex variability in tight-knittedness and status centralization suggests that these indexes may be useful in clarifying peer influence processes for both girls and boys. For example, is peer influence stronger among youth who are members of tightly knit groups? Are group structures less relevant in networks with relatively indistinct groups? Whether these processes are similar for girls and boys, we are likely to learn something important about how structural features of peer groups and networks may moderate the process of peer influence.

References

Adler, P. A. (1996). Preadolescent clique stratification and the hierarchy of identity. *Sociological Inquiry, 66*(2), 111–142.

Adler, P. A., & Adler, P. (1996). Dynamics of inclusion and exclusion in preadolescent cliques. *Social Psychology Quarterly, 58*(3), 145–162.

Adler, P., Kless, S., & Adler, P. (1992). Socialization to gender roles: Popularity among elementary school boys and girls. *Sociology of Education, 65*(3), 169–187.

Benenson, J. F. (1990). Gender differences in social networks. *Journal of Early Adolescence, 10*(4), 472–495.
Benenson, J. F. (1993). Greater preference among females than males for dyadic interaction in early childhood. *Child Development, 64*(2), 544–555.
Benenson, J. F., Apostoleris, N. H., & Parnass, J. (1997). Age and sex differences in dyadic and group interaction. *Developmental Psychology, 33*, 538–543.
Bonacich, P. (1987). Power and centrality: A family of measures. *American Journal of Sociology, 92*(5), 1170–1182.
Borgatti, S. P. (2005). Centrality and network flow. *Social Networks, 27*(1), 55–71.
Cairns, R. B., Cairns, B. D., Neckerman, H. J., Gest, S. D., & Gariepy, J. L. (1988). Social networks and aggressive behavior: Peer support or peer rejection? *Developmental Psychology, 24*(6), 815–823.
Cairns, R. B., Perrin, J. E., & Cairns, B. D. (1985). Social structure and social cognition in early adolescence: Affiliative patterns. *Journal of Early Adolescence, 5*, 339–355.
Charlesworth, W. R., & Dzur, C. (1987). Gender comparisons of preschoolers' behavior and resource utilization in group problem solving. *Child Development, 58*(1), 191–200.
Coleman, J. S. (1961). *The adolescent society: The social life of the teenager and its impact on education.* New York: Free Press.
Crosnoe, R., & Needham, B. (2004). Holism, contextual variability, and the study of friendships in adolescent development. *Child Development, 75*(1), 264–279.
Dunphy, D. C. (1963). The social structure of urban adolescent peer groups. *Sociometry, 26*(2), 230–246.
Eder, D., & Hallinan, M. T. (1978). Sex differences in children's friendships. *American Sociological Review, 43*(2), 237–250.
Fabes, R. A., Martin, C. L., & Hanish, L. D. (2003). Qualities of young children's same-, other-, and mixed-sex play. *Child Development, 74*(3), 921–932.
Freeman, L. C. (1972). Segregation in social networks. *Sociological Methods and Research, 6*, 411–430.
Freeman, L. C. (1979). Centrality in social networks: Conceptual clarification. *Social Networks, 1*, 215–239.
Gest, S. D., Farmer, T. W., Cairns, B. D., & Xie, H. (2003). Identifying children's peer social networks in school classrooms: Links between peer reports and observed interactions. *Social Development, 12*(4), 513–529.
Gest, S. D., Moody, J., & Rulison, K. L. (2007). Density or distinction? The roles of data structure and group detection methods in describing adolescent peer groups. *Journal of Social Structure, 8*(1). Retrieved October 8, 2007, from http://www.cmu.edu/joss/content/articles/volume8/GestMoody/.
Gest, S. D., Rulison, K. L., Davidson, A. J., & Welsh, J. A. (in press). A reputation for success (or failure): The association of peer academic reputations with academic self-concept, effort and performance across the upper elementary grades. *Developmental Psychology*.
Goodwin, M. H. (2002). Exclusion in girls' peer groups: Ethnographic analysis of language practices on the playground. *Human Development, 45*(6), 392–415.
Hallinan, M. T. (1980). Patterns of cliquing among youth. In H. C. Foot, A. J. Chapman, & J. R. Smith (Eds.), *Friendship and social relations in children* (pp. 321–342). New Brunswick, NJ: Transaction Publishers.
Handcock, M. S., Hunter, D. R., Butts, C. T., Goodreau, S. M., & Morris, M. (2003). *Statnet: An R package for the statistical modeling of social networks.* Retrieved October 8, 2007, from http://www.csde.washington.edu/statnet.
Ladd, G. W. (1983). Social networks of popular, average, and rejected children in school settings. *Merrill-Palmer Quarterly, 29*(3), 283–307.
Leaper, C. (Ed.). (1994). *Childhood gender segregation: Causes and consequences.* San Francisco: Jossey-Bass.

Leaper, C., & Smith, T. (2004). A meta-analytic review of gender variations in children's language use: Talkativeness, affiliative speech, and assertive speech. *Developmental Psychology, 40*(6), 993–1027.

Maccoby, E. E. (1990). Gender and relationships: A developmental account. *American Psychologist, 45*(4), 513–520.

Maccoby, E. E. (1998). *The two sexes: Growing up apart, coming together.* Cambridge, MA: Harvard University Press.

Maccoby, E. E., & Jacklin, C. N. (1974). *The psychology of sex differences.* Stanford, CA: Stanford University Press.

Merten, D. E. (1995).The meaning of meanness: Popularity, competition and conflict among junior high school girls. *Sociology of Education, 70*(3), 175–191.

Merten, D. E. (2005). Transitions and "trouble": Rites of passage for suburban girls. *Anthropology and Education Quarterly, 36*(2), 132–148.

Moody, J. (2000). *SPAN: SAS programs for analyzing networks.* Chapel Hill: University of North Carolina.

Omark, D. R., & Edelman, M. S. (1975). A comparison of status hierarchies in young children: An ethological approach. *Social Science Information, 14*(5), 87–107.

Parker, J. G., & Asher, S. R. (1987). Peer relations and later personal adjustment: Are low-accepted children at risk? *Psychological Bulletin, 102,* 357–389.

Parker, J. G., & Seal, J. (1996). Forming, losing, renewing, and replacing friendships: Applying temporal parameters to the assessment of children's friendship experiences. *Child Development, 67*(5), 2248–2268.

Rose, A. J., & Rudolph, K. D. (2006). A review of sex differences in peer relationship processes: Potential trade-offs for the emotional and behavioral development of girls and boys. *Psychological Bulletin, 132*(1), 98–131.

Savin-Williams, R. C. (1979). Dominance hierarchies in groups of early adolescents. *Child Development, 50*(4), 923–935.

Savin-Williams, R. C. (1980). Dominance hierarchies in groups of middle to late adolescent males. *Journal of Youth and Adolescence, 9*(1), 75–85.

Scott, J. (2000). *Social network analysis: A handbook.* Thousand Oaks, CA: Sage.

Sebanc, A. M., Pearce, S. L., Cheatham, C. L., & Gunnar, M. R. (2003). Gendered social worlds in preschool: Dominance, peer acceptance and assertive social skills in boys' and girls' peer groups. *Social Development, 12*(1), 91–106.

Smith, A. B., & Inder, P. M. (1993). Social interaction in same and cross gender pre-school peer groups: A participant observation study. *Educational Psychology, 13*(1), 29–42.

Strayer, F. F., & Strayer, J. (1976). An ethological analysis of social agonism and dominance relations among preschool children. *Child Development, 47*(4), 980–989.

Thorne, B. (1993). *Gender play: Girls and boys in school.* New Brunswick, NJ: Rutgers University Press.

Underwood, M. (2004). Gender and peer relations: Are the two gender cultures really all that different? In J. B. Kupersmidt & K. A. Dodge (Eds.), *Children's peer relations: From development to intervention: Decade of behavior* (pp. 21–36). Washington, DC: American Psychological Association.

Wasserman, S., & Faust, K. (1994). *Social network analysis: Methods and applications.* Cambridge: Cambridge University Press.

SCOTT D. GEST *is associate professor of human development and family studies at the Pennsylvania State University.*

ALICE J. DAVIDSON *is a doctoral candidate in the Human Development and Family Studies program at the Pennsylvania State University.*

KELLY L. RULISON *is a doctoral candidate in the Human Development and Family Studies program at the Pennsylvania State University.*

JAMES MOODY *is associate professor of sociology at Duke University.*

JANET A. WELSH *is a research associate at the Prevention Research Center for the Promotion of Human Development at the Pennsylvania State University.*

The authors use p* modeling to explore connections between network structures and social influence in a seventh-grade friendship network. Specifically, p* parameters reveal how bullying perpetration, dyads, triads, and more complex group structures contribute to network formation, providing fine-level detail about the operation of internal peer group structures.

Statistical Analysis of Friendship Patterns and Bullying Behaviors Among Youth

Dorothy L. Espelage, Harold D. Green Jr., Stanley Wasserman

During adolescence, friendship affiliations and groups provide companionship and social and emotional support, and they afford opportunities for intimate self-disclosure and reflection (McNelles & Connolly, 1999). Friendships often promote positive psychosocial development, but some youth learn and adopt antisocial attitudes and deviant behaviors through their friendships (see Gifford-Smith, Dodge, Dishion, & McCord, 2005; Chapter Six, this volume). Frequent, longer-term, and close associations with deviant peers are strongly correlated with adolescents' own deviant behavior (Loeber & Dishion, 1987; Loeber & Stouthamer-Loeber, 1986; Patterson, Dishion, & Yoerger, 2000; Vitaro, Brendgen, & Tremblay, 2000; Warr, 2002). Peers influence attitudes and behaviors by acting as role models (Kaplan, Johnson, & Bailey, 1987), reinforcing deviant behavior (Esbensen & Deschenes, 1998), and developing mutually influential norms that promote continued deviant behavior (Dishion, Patterson, & Griesler, 1994; Loeber & Dishion, 1987).

Clearly peers matter, but can the monolith of peer group effects be deconstructed in a way that advances theories of peer influence? To date, sociologists, criminologists, and developmental psychologists have relied consistently on tabulating the number of deviant friends that a child or adolescent is exposed to and correlating this figure with the target child's own

self-reported deviant behavior. More recently researchers have begun to use social network analysis to identify global friendship structures (cliques) and local structures (dyads) to examine several theories of peer influence (Espelage, Holt, & Henkel, 2003; Xu, Farver, Schwartz, & Chang, 2004). However, these methods fail to examine the building blocks of these peer groups beyond the dyad, and with few exceptions, they have virtually ignored how positions that children and adolescents hold within a peer group affect their susceptibility to influence or their development of antisocial attitudes and behaviors (Haynie, 2001). Thus, this chapter represents an important contribution to the peer relations literature by using statistical models to demonstrate how adolescent friendship structures grow into dyads, triads, and tetrads (groups of four) and then possibly into larger entities, and how peer effects can be examined within these structures.

Although there are many applications to the models used in this chapter, bullying perpetration was selected as the major outcome for several reasons. First, Ojala and Nesdale (2004) adapted social identity theory (Tajfel & Turner, 1979) and established that attitudes toward bullying are derived from and maintained through group norms. The investigators presented to children eight versions of a scenario in which they manipulated the main character's behavior (for example, bullying and helping), the character's group norms, and attributions of the target of character's behavior. Children behaved in accordance with their group's norms. For example, bullies were more likely to be accepted or retained as a group member if their group had a positive attitude toward bullying. Second, many bullying episodes involve the active and passive participation of multiple individuals within and across groups. Salmivalli and colleagues (Salmivalli, Lagerspetz, Björkqvist, Österman, & Kaukiainen, 1996; Salmivalli & Voeten, 2004) have identified that students can perpetrate the bullying, while others either assist or reinforce the bully. Third, bullying perpetration is also an excellent focus of this chapter because peer groups play an important role in explanatory models of bullying, including attraction theory (Bukowski, Sippola, & Newcomb, 2000), dominance theory (Pellegrini, 2002), and the homophily hypothesis (Cairns, Cairns, Neckerman, Gest, & Gariepy, 1988; Espelage et al., 2003). The homophily hypothesis is discussed more fully as it is the focus of this chapter.

According to the homophily hypothesis, individuals within the same group are likely to report similar attitudes and engagement in similar forms of behavior as a result of self-selection, peer socialization, or the combined effects of both factors (Kandel, 1978). *Self-selection* refers to individuals' selecting to be friends with others who already hold similar attitudes or participate in similar behaviors. *Socialization* refers to the process by which individuals within the group influence each other and internalize the norms established by the group (Eder & Nenga, 2003; McPerson, Smith-Lovin, & Cook, 2001). Support for the homophily hypothesis has been documented in the bullying literature through the application of social network analysis (SNA; Espelage et al., 2003; Poteat, Espelage, & Green,

2007). Espelage and colleagues (2003) used SNA to identify peer cliques and dyads and employed hierarchical linear modeling to determine the extent to which peers influenced each other in relation to changes in bullying. Overall, middle school students tended to hang out with students who bullied at similar frequencies, and students who hung out with children who bullied others increased their amount of self-reported bullying over the school year. In a more recent investigation, Poteat, Espelage, and Green (2007) found support for the homophily hypothesis in adolescent peer groups on individuals' heterosexist and social dominance attitudes. SNA was used to identify peer groups, and group socialization effects on individuals' social dominance attitudes were observed. The documented social influence of the group, in addition to self-selection, suggests a more active role of peer group members in accounting for individuals' own bullying behavior than would be suggested based on self-selection alone. These studies call for continued efforts to unpack peer group contextual effects on bullying perpetration.

Recent advances in statistical modeling of network structures make it possible to approach the problem from a perspective more analogous to the development of peer groups. Social groups begin with individuals and grow into dyads, triads, tetrads, and possibly larger entities. New statistical approaches model the relationships between network structure and individual behaviors and attitudes, starting from the assumption that all structures and behaviors are stochastic across a network (that is, individuals are random and may or may not be affected by social structures). From there, the significance of dyadic structures, triadic structures, starlike (or popularity) structures, and other higher-order structural parameters is investigated, with each parameter conditioned on all other parameters previously included in the model. This approach, which began with p_1 (dyadic independence) and p_2 (dyadic independence with heterogeneous parameters depending on actor covariates) modeling has evolved into a more sophisticated approach using the exponential family of random graph distributions, known as p^*. These models allow us to break monolithic peer groups into their building blocks and provide a more sophisticated understanding of the mechanisms associated with homophily (or other social influence mechanisms). These modeling approaches have been enabled most strongly by developments in statistical estimation, well known in the literature as maximum likelihood Markov chain Monte Carlo (MCMC) simulation (Wasserman & Robins, 2005) and applied within the past several years to networks. Wasserman and Robins (2005, p. 5) argue that p^* analyses enable "an effective and informed move from local, micro phenomena to overall, macro phenomena." Thus, for the problem at hand, p^* analyses allow us to model homophily processes at the microlevel in ways that allow us to gain an overall understanding of their effects among children. (Of note, SIENA, pnet, and statnet are the most popular software tools used for p^* modeling. See Chapter Six, this volume, on SIENA.)

Method

To explore the complex structure of adolescents' peer networks and the ways in which bullying behavior is distributed across networks, we studied middle schoolers' friendship networks.

Participants. For the purposes of demonstrating the use of p^* analyses to examine friendship patterns and bullying perpetration, data from the seventh-grade class from a midwestern school were used. These data were drawn from a larger data set. The participants were 81 male and 107 female seventh-grade students ($N = 188$) whose ages ranged from twelve through fourteen years ($M = 12.74$, $SD = .54$). Approximately 94 percent were Caucasian, 0.5 percent were African American, 0.5 percent were Asian, 4.3 percent were biracial, and 0.7 percent reported other racial backgrounds.

Procedure. Participants completed the study survey during a forty-five-minute free period. Surveys were administered to groups ranging in size from seven to fifteen students. Students sat such that they were not close to one another. Once students were arranged, the project was introduced to them. They were informed that they would be asked questions about aggression, their feelings, and their friends. They were told that they would receive a pencil and a highlighter for their participation and would be eligible for a drawing for a ten dollar gift certificate for a local music store or bookstore. The drawing was conducted at the end of the survey administration in each classroom. Students were asked to give their written consent by signing their name on the front cover sheet and confidentiality and anonymity were assured. In each classroom, one of two trained examiners read each item and response option aloud while a second team member monitored students' progress. Students were allowed to ask questions if they had difficulty understanding any words.

Measures. The survey consisted of three sections: demographic questions, the bullying perpetration scale, and the friendship nomination task.

Demographic Variables. Self-reports of sex, grade, and race were elicited to determine demographic characteristics.

Bullying Assessment. The nine-item Illinois Bully Scale (Espelage & Holt, 2001) was used to assess the frequency of teasing, name-calling, social exclusion, and rumor spreading. This scale is a modified version of the Aggression Scale (Orpinas & Frankowski, 2001). Students are asked how often in the past thirty days they had teased other students, upset other students for the fun of it, excluded others from their group of friends, and helped harass other students. Response options were "never," "1 or 2 times," "3 or 4 times," "5 or 6 times," and "7 or more times." The construct validity of this scale has been supported by exploratory and confirmatory factor analysis (Espelage & Holt, 2001). The scale consistently emerges as distinct from physical aggression scales (Espelage & Holt, 2001; Espelage et al., 2003). A Cronbach alpha coefficient of .87 was found for this sample.

Friendship Nomination Task. Students were asked to list from one to eight friends similar in age (but not their siblings) with whom they "hang out with most often in their school." These instructions followed the guidelines of Ennett and Bauman (1994, 1996). The names were then converted to participant numbers and matched with survey data.

Data Analytic Strategy and Study Hypotheses

As in previous analyses of this sort (Espelage et al., 2003; Poteat et al., 2007), only confirmed (mutual or reciprocal) ties between children were used in this analysis. Rather than grouping students into bullying ranges, the bully perpetration scale was maintained as a continuous variable in an effort to avoid manipulating the data and to represent the self-reported behaviors more closely.

The p^* models were calculated using the PNET program (Wang, Robins, & Pattison, 2006), which allows conditional, MCMC modeling of structural and behavioral parameters of networks. The hypotheses tested were based on homophily theories, balance theories, and theories of group and collective action, though models that represent other structural and behavioral theories could just as easily have been specified. Figure 5.1 presents diagrams that define the structural parameters discussed in the following hypotheses.

HYPOTHESIS 0. *Random distribution of friendship ties.*

Children will choose their friends without respect to the structural and behavioral characteristics of their potential friends or themselves. Thus, the global null hypothesis is that all structural and behavioral parameters included in the p^* statistical model will be nonsignificant. In the following

Figure 5.1. Diagrams of Structures Associated with Model Parameters

Parameter Name	Parameter Diagram
Edges	
K-Star (K = 3)	
Alternating K-Triangles (K = 3)	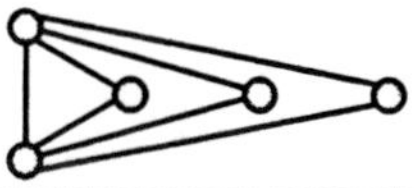

Source: Based on Wang, Robins, & Pattison (2006).

specific cases, null hypotheses are that the network will not display a particular structural signature more or less often than chance. In other words, children will not form friendship ties that create the hypothesized patterns. This corresponds to a nonsignificant or zero parameter estimate in the models. The following alternative hypotheses were tested:

HYPOTHESIS 1. *Friendships are expensive.*

Friendships require investments of time, effort, and social capital. Thus, children will create friendship ties only in the presence of other structural or behavioral factors that encourage friendship ties to form. It is hypothesized that children will form friendships less frequently than predicted by chance. This will be reflected in the p^* model as a significant negative parameter for edges.

HYPOTHESIS 2. *A friend of a friend is my friend.*

Because of pressures to form cliques, it is believed that children will form triangular friendship groups. However, it is important to note that triangles are only the building blocks of larger social groups, and thus it is also postulated that children will form a friendship tie if it closes multiple paths of length two into multiple triangles with common vertices. It is hypothesized that children will form these triangle-closing relationships more frequently than predicted by chance and that paths of length two (called 2-Stars in the p^* vocabulary) will occur less frequently than by chance. This will be reflected in the p^* model as a significant negative parameter for 2-Stars.

HYPOTHESIS 3. *Popular children affect network structure.*

Popularity among seventh graders underlies the development of groups in that those who are popular are often involved in large, closely connected groups. Thus, it is hypothesized that popular children will become centers for other clusters of children who are interconnected in stars, triangles, and other higher-order structures that form the basis of cliques and other social groups. More specifically, it is hypothesized that children will form relationships with popular children more frequently than predicted by chance. This will be reflected in the p^* model as a significant positive parameter for 1-Stars.

HYPOTHESIS 4. *Cliques are important.*

Peer groups are important and comprise a large amount of social structure seen among school children. These peer groups are represented as triangles in a network graph. However, triangles are only the building blocks of larger (and more important) transitive peer group structures composed of multiple closed triangles that share vertices. Extending hypotheses 2 and 3, we hypothesize that children will have a higher probability of forming a tie when it increases the number of closed, transitive triangles that share edges in common. This is represented in the model as a positive alternating K-triangle parameter. Here "alternating" implies a particular pattern associated with the frequency of these triangles, controlling for other lower-level triangle effects. We hypothesize that children will form these relationships more frequently than predicted by chance. This will be reflected in the p^* model as a significant positive parameter for Alternating 2-Triangles.

HYPOTHESIS 5. *Birds of a feather flock together.*

Homophily theories suggest that children who share similar attitudinal and behavioral characteristics will be friends with each other. Homophily behaviors are represented in this model by two parameters: a "sum" parameter (calculated by summing the scores associated with the children in each dyad), which, when positive, implies that those with high scores group together, and a "difference" parameter (calculated by taking the absolute value of the difference between the scores associated with the children in each dyad), which, when negative, suggests that those with differing scores do not group together. It is hypothesized that children will form homophilous relationships more frequently than predicted by chance. This will be reflected in the p^* model as a significant positive parameter for Sum of Bullying Perpetration Scale and as a significant negative parameter for Difference of Bullying Perpetration Scale.

Results

This section presents the results of the MCMC p^* modeling of the seventh-grade friendship network, including scores on the bullying perpetration scale as a behavioral attribute for each adolescent. The correct interpretation of these parameters requires the investigation of three features: the parameter, its standard deviation, and the associated convergence t-statistic. The convergence t-statistic measures how well the model fits the data. The sign of a parameter estimate provides an indication of whether a particular structural feature occurs more or less often than predicted by chance. The standard deviation of the parameter assesses the significance of the parameter in the model. If the parameter estimate is greater than two times the standard deviation, it represents a significant effect. Table 5.1 reports these measures for the proposed model, in which all six parameters were significant, which leads to rejection of each of the null hypotheses. These structural and behavioral signatures all occur more or less frequently than predicted by chance.

Model Interpretation. For a model to be considered well fitted, the t-statistics must be near zero (generally less than 0.1 in absolute value). In this case, the t-statistic = (parameter observation—sample mean)/standard deviation, providing an average value of how well a parameter, when estimated through the MCMC procedure, matches the parameter in the

Table 5.1. Parameter Estimates

Parameter Name	Parameter Estimate	Standard Deviation	Convergence t-Statistic
Edges	−4.72	0.59	0.012
K-2-Star	−1.07	0.21	0.011
K-1-Star	1.27	0.56	0.014
Alternating Transitive K-2-Triangles	1.85	0.087	−0.023
Sum of bullying scale	0.14	0.054	−0.018
Difference of bullying scale	−0.67	0.093	−0.067

observed graphs. All of the parameters included in this model are below the convergence threshold, suggesting that the model fits the data well. This allows the testing of hypotheses associated with specific parameters. These models are conditional, meaning that each subsequent parameter added to the model represents a mechanism that is operating over and above other mechanisms. This suggests multiple mechanisms are operating in the social environment. Thus, structural mechanisms are examined first, starting with basic dyadic parameters, and then triadic parameters followed by cliques. Behavioral similarity (homophily) and its relation to social structure are examined in the final analyses:

- Hypothesis 1. A significant, negative parameter (estimate = −4.72) for edges (friendship) suggests that in general, forming new relationships is costly. Children are unlikely to create new friendships in the absence of other structural or behavioral catalysts.
- Hypothesis 2. The significant, negative 2-Star (multiple paths of length two with a shared intermediary) parameter (estimate = −1.07) supported the hypothesis that youth will create friendship ties that create triangular structures and close open paths of length two. Thus, paths of length two occur less often than predicted by chance. In other words, the friends of my friend will become my friends.
- Hypothesis 3. The 1-Star (popularity) parameter is positive and significant (estimate = 1.27). This supports the hypothesis that youth are more likely to form friendships with highly popular individuals than expected by chance and are less likely to form friendships with more isolated individuals. Popular children *do* affect the structure of the friendship network.
- Hypothesis 4. The Alternating 2-Triangles (multiple edgewise shared partners) parameter is significant and positive (estimate = 1.85). Over and above the triangle closure predicted in hypothesis 2, children form friendship ties that create multiple closed triangles more often than expected by chance. This suggests that multiple edgewise shared partners, the building blocks of cliques, affinity groups, or peer groups, affect the probability of a

Figure 5.2. Network of Seventh-Grade Participants' Friendship Ties

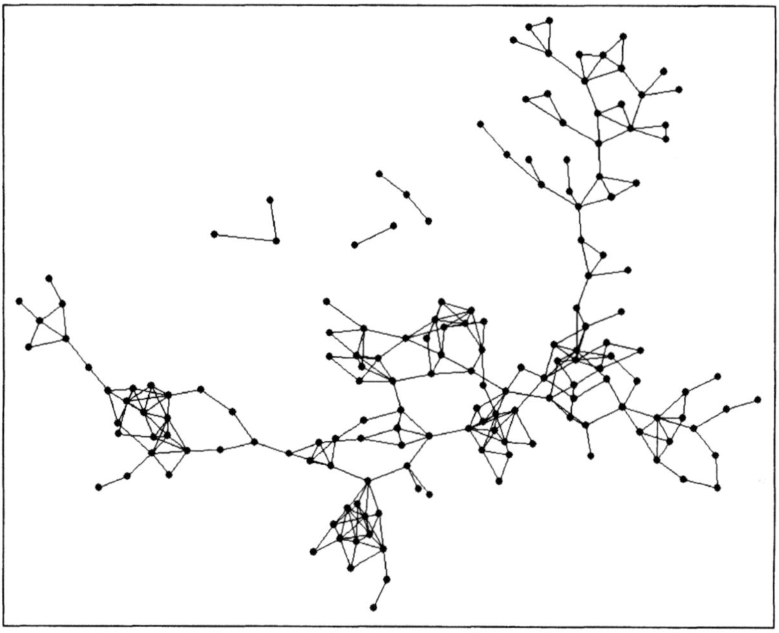

tie being formed in this network. At the network level, this means that ties among children tend to clump together into denser regions of the graph. Cliques clearly are important!

In combination, the negative 2-Star and positive Alternating 2-Triangle parameters suggest a filigreed pattern in the network, such that relationships are not concentrated among a few individuals but are spread among all children to some degree. This additional effect was not hypothesized but is an outcome of the interaction of these parameters within a network. Figure 5.2 presents the seventh-grade network with isolates removed. It presents a filigreed pattern, suggesting that the proposed models reflect the data fairly well.

The structural hypotheses reflect mechanisms that build from the individual through the dyad and the triad to the clique. The remaining hypothesis investigates the importance of behavioral influence in the creation of friendships, revealing how behaviors, attitudes, and attributes modify the basic structural mechanisms. Specifically, the relation between similarity in bullying behavior and different social structures is investigated:

- Hypothesis 5. A significant, positive sum parameter (estimate = 0.14) suggests that children who score high on the bullying perpetration scale (and thus bully more frequently) tend to have ties to each other more often than expected by chance. Bullies are friends with bullies and nonbullies with nonbullies. A significant, negative difference parameter (estimate = –0.67) suggests that children who score differently on the bullying perpetration scale are less likely to have ties to each other than expected by chance. Bullies and nonbullies are not often friends.

Based on the study hypotheses, which focus on dyads, triads, and other small structural units, it could be argued that the p^* approach is reductionist. Although it is true that p^* analyses approach the investigation of peer groups from the bottom up, it is not necessarily considered reductionist. When the parameters given in Table 5.1 are used to simulate networks of the same size, the re-creation of the observed networks is almost perfect. In other words, the model fits the data very well, without losing much structural information or reducing the network to a simpler form. The results of these simulations are presented in Table 5.2. Because the number of simulated graphs is not a thousand but a million, a parameter with a t-statistic less than two is acceptable. Networks were simulated based on the significant parame-

Table 5.2. Goodness-of-Fit Information

	Initial Parameter Values		
Edge	–4.72		
K-2-Stars	–1.07		
K-1-Stars	1.27		
K-2 Triangles	1.85		
Sum of bullying scale	0.14		
Difference of bullying scale	–0.67		

	Observed Network Statistics	Simulated Statistic Mean	Simulated Statistic Standard Deviation	Observed t-Statistics
Edge	290	282.21	22.15	0.35
K-2-Stars	604.78	577.29	71.35	0.39
K-1-Stars	413	397.7	41.68	0.37
Alternating K-Triangles	274.25	262.65	35.11	0.33
Sum of Bullying Scale	958.76	927.88	70.21	0.44
Difference of Bullying Scale	148.2	143.22	14.65	0.34
Standard deviation of degree distribution	2.05	2.03	0.15	0.13
Skew of degree distribution	0.38	0.63	0.18	–1.38
Global clustering	0.37	0.34	0.023	1.48
Average local clustering	0.34	0.34	0.03	–0.9
Variance local clustering	0.11	0.12	0.013	–0.95

ters from our model. The simulated networks matched the observed network on all ten of the network statistics calculated for goodness of fit. This suggests that the few parameters we entered were able to recreate the entirety of the network structure with very little loss of information.

Discussion

From an ecological perspective, child and adolescent attitudes and behavior are believed to be shaped by a range of contextual systems, including family, peers, school, and communities (Bronfenbrenner, 1979). Peer groups are considered a microsystem because they contain members who have direct contact and bidirectional interactions. Unfortunately, the understanding of how peers influence their friends' attitudes and behaviors has been limited to basic descriptive analyses. That is, what is known is that children and adolescents are socialized by their friends, but very little research has examined how, when, and under what conditions influence varies.

An important first step in beginning to document the impact of peer groups on social behavior is a closer consideration of friendship patterns. In this chapter, we demonstrated that p^* modeling techniques could be used to examine mechanisms associated with the theories of homophily and efficiently investigate the impact of dyadic, triadic, and higher-order social structures on the friendship networks observed among the seventh graders in this study. Homophilous dyads, triads, and stars were found to be significant building blocks of the friendship groups, and all served as microlevel mechanisms that motivate the macrolevel construct of peer group effects. Our p^* modeling techniques allowed us to break peer groups apart, shedding light on how they operate. The findings support propositions concerning the importance of reciprocated ties, popularity, triangular structures, and homophily when assessing the social behavior of these children. Results of this investigation also highlight the importance of moving beyond the common practice among developmentalists of focusing solely on dyads—the lowest level of social structure—and cliques—the highest level of social structure—toward an examination of those structures that lie in between (Haynie, 2001).

Due to limited space, only a few hypotheses can be tested with the models we presented. Thus, it is important to consider extensions of the models presented here in an effort to call attention to the wide array of social theories that may be tested in using this framework. First, this model could be extended to include other behavioral, demographic, and attitudinal information, including sex, ethnicity, attitudes toward bullying, measures of aggressive behavior, and bully-victim status. Second, the model evaluated included relational ties between children only when both children noted the relationship. A less restrictive alternative would be to model the graph that allows relational ties when either child noted the relationship. The motivation is that the social reality would lie somewhere in the intervening space.

Analyses included investigating the impact of homophily in shaping bullying perpetration. Children tended to be friends with others who shared similar levels of bullying perpetration. This finding is consistent with previous work indicating that positive attitudes toward bullying emerge within the social context of peer groups (Ojala & Nesdale, 2004) and bullying perpetration levels are similar among friends (Espelage et al., 2003).

The homophily hypothesis is only one of several peer influence theories that could be evaluated using social network and friendship pattern analyses. For example, attraction theory postulates that adolescents are attracted to aggressive peers because they represent an important step toward independence (Bukowski et al., 2000). In addition, dominance is being used more and more as an organizational framework to understand bullying perpetration. From this perspective, bullying is a means by which to establish dominance hierarchies among peers, such that certain individuals eventually attain a higher status, more access to resources, and greater control or influence over other peers (Bjorklund & Pellegrini, 2002; Boulton, 1992; Pellegrini & Long, 2002). Applications of social network analysis and models testing dominance theory like those employed in this chapter are sparse. However, given that dominance status can be attained through either affiliative (for example, leadership) or antagonistic (for example, bullying) methods (Hawley, 1999; Lease, Musgrove, & Axelrod, 2002), research in this area could benefit from using analyses to reconstruct friendship patterns like the methods used in this chapter. Overall, future research is needed to examine how friendship patterns are related to attraction levels and dominance shifts as a function of friendship structures.

Although this chapter included the negative behavior of bullying perpetration, peer groups can also have a positive influence on youth. For example, students who perceive greater peer social support tend to be uninvolved in bullying (Demaray & Malecki, 2001). Also, in another study, peer victimization was not linked to internalizing and externalizing behavior problems for youth with sufficient social support (Hodges & Perry, 1999). Furthermore, peers can promote positive social functioning among youth; adolescents with low levels of prosocial behaviors in sixth grade relative to their friends demonstrated improved prosocial behaviors at the end of eighth grade (Wentzel & Caldwell, 1997). Just as the homophily hypothesis can explain similarities in peer group aggression, it also can explain similarities in prosocial interactions. In addition to these areas of interest, many questions remain about peer influences on bullying perpetration. For example, questions like the following remain: Is influence equivalent in a peer group of three members versus a peer group of seven members? If a peer group is made up of many popular members versus just one popular member, does influence vary across these two groups? In other words, how does the cohesiveness of a group moderate peer influence? How, specifically, do the structures associated with peer group social behavior influence changes in attitudes and beliefs? Fortunately, major progress is being made in the development of statistical models to address many of these questions. This chapter is an important demonstration of how new developments in social network methodologies are allowing social scientists to enter more closely into adolescent social groups and more closely examine influence over time.

References

Bjorklund, D. F., & Pellegrini, A. D. (2002). *The origins of human nature: Evolutionary developmental psychology.* Washington, DC: American Psychological Association.

Boulton, M. J. (1992). Rough physical play in adolescents: Does it serve a dominance function? *Early Education and Development, 3,* 312–333.

Bronfenbrenner, U. (1979). *The ecology of human development: Experiments by nature and design.* Cambridge, MA: Harvard University Press.

Bukowski, W. M., Sippola, L. K., & Newcomb, A. F. (2000). Variations in patterns of attraction to same- and other-sex peers during early adolescence. *Developmental Psychology, 36,* 147–154.

Cairns, R. B., Cairns, B. D., Neckerman, H. J., Gest, S. D., & Gariepy, J. L. (1988). Social networks and aggressive behavior: Peer support or peer rejection? *Developmental Psychology, 24*(6), 815–823.

Demaray, M. K., & Malecki, C. K. (2001). Importance ratings of socially supportive behaviors by children and adolescents. *School Psychology Review, 32,* 108–131.

Dishion, T. J., Patterson, G. R., & Griesler, P. C. (1994). Peer adaptations in the development of antisocial behavior: A confluence model. In L. R. Huesmann (Ed.), *Aggressive behavior: Current perspectives* (pp. 61–95). New York: Plenum.

Eder, D., & Nenga, S. K. (2003). Socialization in adolescence. In J. Delamater (Ed.), *Handbook of social psychology* (pp. 157–182). New York: Kluwer.

Ennett, S. T., & Bauman, K. E. (1994). The contribution of influence and selection to adolescent peer group homogeneity: The case of adolescent cigarette smoking. *Journal of Personality and Social Psychology, 67,* 653–663.

Ennett, S. T., & Bauman, K. E. (1996). Adolescent social networks: School, demographic, and longitudinal considerations. *Journal of Adolescent Research, 11,* 194–215.

Esbensen, F. A., & Deschenes, E. P. (1998). A multisite examination of youth gang membership: Does gender matter? *Criminology, 36,* 799–827.

Espelage, D. L., & Holt, M. L. (2001). Bullying and victimization during early adolescence: Peer influences and psychosocial correlates. *Journal of Emotional Abuse, 2*(3), 123–142.

Espelage, D. L., Holt, M., & Henkel, R. (2003). Examination of peer-group contextual effects on aggression during early adolescence. *Child Development, 74,* 205–220.

Gifford-Smith, M., Dodge, K. A., Dishion, T. J., & McCord, J. (2005). Peer influence in children and adolescents: Crossing the bridge from developmental to intervention science. *Journal of Abnormal Child Psychology, 33,* 255–265.

Hawley, P. H. (1999). The ontogenesis of social dominance: A strategy-based evolutionary perspective. *Developmental Review, 19,* 97–132.

Haynie, D. L. (2001). Delinquent peers revisited: Does network structure matter? *American Journal of Sociology, 106,* 1013–1057.

Hodges, E.V.E., & Perry, D. G. (1999). Personal and interpersonal antecedents and consequences of victimization by peers. *Journal of Personality and Social Psychology, 76,* 677–685.

Kandel, D. B. (1978). Homophily, selection, and socialization in adolescent friendships. *American Journal of Sociology, 84,* 427–436.

Kaplan, H. B., Johnson, R. J., & Bailey, C. A. (1987). Deviant peers and deviant behavior: Further elaboration of a model. *Social Psychology Quarterly, 50,* 277–284.

Lease, M. L., Musgrove, K. T., & Axelrod, J. L. (2002). Dimensions of social status in preadolescent peer groups: Likability, perceived popularity, and social dominance. *Social Development, 11,* 508–533.

Loeber, R., & Dishion, T. J. (1987). Antisocial and delinquent youths: Methods for their early identification. In J. D. Burchard & S. Burchard (Eds.), *Prevention of delinquent behavior* (pp. 75–89). Thousand Oaks, CA: Sage.

Loeber, R., & Stouthamer-Loeber, M. (1986). Family factors as correlates and predictors of juvenile conduct problems and delinquency. In M. Tonry & N. Morris (Eds.), *Crime and justice* (Vol. 7, pp. 29–149). Chicago: University of Chicago Press.

McNelles, L. R., & Connolly, J. A. (1999). Intimacy between adolescent friends: Age and gender differences in intimate affect and intimate behaviors. *Journal of Research on Adolescence, 9,* 143-159.

McPerson, M., Smith-Lovin, L., & Cook, J. M. (2001). Birds of a feather: Homophily in social networks. *Annual Review of Sociology, 27,* 415–444.

Ojala, K., & Nesdale, D. (2004). Bullying and social identity: The effects of group norms and distinctiveness threat on attitudes towards bullying. *British Journal of Developmental Psychology, 22,* 19–35.

Orpinas, P., & Frankowski, R. (2001). The Aggression Scale: A self-report measure of aggressive behavior for young adolescents. *Journal of Early Adolescence, 21,* 50–67.

Patterson, G. R., Dishion, T. J., & Yoerger, K. (2000). Adolescent growth in new forms of problem behavior: Macro- and micro-peer dynamics. *Prevention Science, 1,* 3–13.

Pellegrini, A. D. (2002). Affiliative and aggressive dimensions of dominance and possible functions during early adolescence. *Aggression and Violent Behavior, 7*(1), 21–31.

Pellegrini, A. D., & Long, J. (2002). A longitudinal study of bullying, dominance, and victimization during the transition from primary to secondary school. *British Journal of Developmental Psychology, 20,* 259–280.

Poteat, P., Espelage, D. L., & Green, H. (2007). The socialization of dominance: Peer group contextual effects on heterosexist and dominance attitudes. *Journal of Personality and Social Psychology 92,* 1040–1050.

Salmivalli, C., Lagerspetz, K., Björkqvist, K., Österman, K., & Kaukiainen, A. (1996). Bullying as a group process: Participant roles and their relations to social status within the group. *Aggressive Behavior, 22,* 1–15.

Salmivalli, C., & Voeten, M. (2004). Connections between attitudes, group norms, and behaviour in bullying situations. *International Journal of Behavioral Development, 28,* 246–258.

Tajfel, H., & Turner, J. C. (1979). The social identity theory of intergroup behavior. In J. T. Jost & J. Sidanius (Eds.), *Political psychology: Key readings in social psychology* (pp. 276–293). New York: Psychology Press.

Vitaro, F., Brendgen, M., & Tremblay, R. E. (2000). Influence of deviant friends on delinquency: Searching for moderator variables. *Journal of Abnormal Child Psychology, 28,* 313–325.

Wang, P., Robins, G., & Pattison, P. (2006). *Pnet: A program for the simulation and estimation of exponential random graph models.* Melbourne: University of Melbourne.

Warr, M. (2002). *Companions in crime: The social aspects of criminal conduct.* Cambridge: Cambridge University Press.

Wasserman, S., & Robins, G. L. (2005). An introduction to random graphs, dependence graphs, and p^*. In P. J. Carrington, J. Scott, & S. Wasserman (Eds.), *Models and methods in social network analysis* (pp. 148–161). Cambridge: Cambridge University Press.

Wentzel, K. R., & Caldwell, K. A. (1997). Friendships, peer acceptance, and group membership: Relations to academic achievement in middle school. *Child Development, 68,* 1198–1209.

Xu, Y., Farver, J.A.M., Schwartz, D., & Chang, L. (2004). Social networks and aggressive behaviour in Chinese children. *International Journal of Behavioral Development, 28*, 401–410.

DOROTHY L. ESPELAGE *is a professor of educational psychology and University Scholar at the University of Illinois at Urbana-Champaign.*

HAROLD D. GREEN JR. *is an associate social and behavioral scientist at RAND Health in Santa Monica, California.*

STANLEY WASSERMAN *is Rudy Professor of Statistics, Psychology, and Sociology at Indiana University, and chair of the Department of Statistics.*

We present an empirical exploration of peer network mechanisms that encourage antisocial behavior in early adolescents. We apply SIENA, a network modeling methodology that addresses developmentally changing, statistically dependent interpersonal friendships.

Early Adolescent Antisocial Behavior and Peer Rejection: A Dynamic Test of a Developmental Process

John M. Light, Thomas J. Dishion

Evidence supports the hypothesis that adolescent peer groups play a significant role in the genesis of youth antisocial behavior (Dishion & Patterson, 2006). A longstanding interest in research focused on individual differences in teen exposure to deviant peer groups is the notion that high-risk youth aggregate because of their common rejection within social contexts, such as the school environment (Cairns, Neckerman, & Cairns, 1989; Dodge et al., 2003; Gifford-Smith, Dodge, Dishion, & McCord, 2005; Olson, 1992). We refer to this dynamic process as the confluence hypothesis (Dishion, Patterson, & Griesler, 1994). The fundamental dynamics are generated by two interrelated processes, selection and influence:

1. Youth at risk for antisocial behavior tend to affiliate differentially with each other (*selection*).
2. These affiliations then increase the risk for higher frequency and severity of such behavior (*influence*).

Two sets of findings provided a major impetus to the surge in peer relationship research in the 1980s. First, investigators recognized that peer

---

NIH grants DA018760–02 and DA13773–05 supported the work on this chapter. We thank Christine Cody for editorial support.

rejection and isolation in childhood were associated with poor adult outcomes (Hartup, 1992). Second, studies showed that peer rejection was a reliable outcome of childhood aggressive behavior (Coie & Kupersmidt, 1983; Dodge, 1983), which furthermore predicted continued aggression several years later (Dodge et al., 2003). Yet this plethora of work provided no convincing case that peer rejection had a causal role in the etiology and course of problem behavior. If peer rejection is causal, what are the mechanisms?

Advances on this issue occurred by crossing boundaries between two disciplines: criminology and developmental psychology. Those studying adolescent delinquency recognized such behavior as a "team activity" (Gold, 1970). Later, systematic longitudinal studies of nationally representative samples revealed deviant peers to be a strong correlate of adolescent delinquency (Elliott, Huizinga, & Ageton, 1985). Considering both developmental and sociological literature led to a paradox: If delinquent youth face peer rejection and lack social skills, why do they belong to normal-sized peer groups (see Farmer & Hollowell, 1994; Farmer, Van Acker, Pearl, & Rodkin, 1999) encouraging their behavior?

The confluence hypothesis emerged to account for the paradox. The idea is simple: deviant peer groups form among mutually rejected youth, who adapt by forming a unique group with a deviant set of mutually influential norms (Dishion et al., 1994). In earlier studies consistent with this hypothesis, we found that peer rejection covaried with more extreme measures of deviant peer involvement in early adolescence. Dishion, Nelson, and Yasui (2005) found sixth-grade peer rejection combined with academic failure to predict eighth-grade male gang involvement, and Rodkin, Farmer, Pearl, and Van Acker (2000) found antisocial males to be most typically (though not invariably) disliked by others.

These studies, while compelling, fell short of a dynamic test of the confluence hypothesis. Primarily the analyses did not consider network embedding. Various factors besides social influence among rejected youth could explain that rejection rates in one year correlate with gang formation two years later. For example, neighborhood could affect both rejection and future gang affiliation. However, analyses by Dishion, Nelson, and Kavanagh (2003) suggested an important principle: each school creates its own peer ecology. Hence, rejection confluence dynamics may vary among schools and need examination within schools. We seek to advance this work by applying a relatively new modeling technique that applies panel-data logic (Kessler & Greenberg, 1981) to peer social ecologies (Snijders, Steglich, Schweinberger, & Huisman, 2007), which we describe in more detail here.

The study of peer group selection and influence effects has benefited from increased reliance on social network methodology. In network studies, we might measure individual-level peer affiliations by asking each member of a relatively closed social group (members of one grade at a school) who their friends are. A number of variations on this procedure are possible (Marsden, 2005). This yields a complete network, that is, a map showing precisely who links to whom. The network approach has two major advantages over other less-specialized methodologies. The first stems from evidence that youth overestimate similarity between themselves and their friends with respect to antisocial behavior (Bauman & Fisher, 1986; Prinstein & Wang, 2007). This can lead to biased estimates of selection and influence effects (Ennett & Bauman, 1994). In network studies, the data point to the friends and the friends' self-reports give a truer assessment of behavior. A second advantage is that networks properly represent "complete" embedding of individuals—that is, their indirect as well as direct relationships—thus reflecting not only an actor's own friends but also the larger context in which this peer group is located.

However, social network modeling presents some methodological challenges. The object is to predict changes in an array of interrelated links, which is beyond the scope of standard statistical methods. Moreover, because network-embedding measures for individuals usually have their basis in overlapping subgroups (Snijders, 2005), individual-level network data are inherently dependent. Ignoring data dependency, even of ostensibly minor magnitude, can produce unpredictable biases in analyses (Kenny & Judd, 1986; Murray & Hannan, 1990). Multilevel modeling is of limited value for longitudinal analysis of such data, moreover, because dependencies change between waves.

Snijders and colleagues developed a statistical modeling methodology, SIENA, for retaining advantages of network methodology while addressing these challenges (Snijders, 2005; Snijders, Steglich & Schweinberger, 2006). SIENA is an open-source program, available free with documentation at http://stat.gamma.rug.nl/stocnet. We describe it further below.

We applied SIENA to test a set of specific hypotheses derived from the social learning-based account of antisocial deviant peer processes outlined above. These hypotheses focused on the parts of antisocial peer dynamics that make the process, by virtue of creating a causal feedback loop.

1. Antisocial behavior predicts peer social marginalization.
2. Marginalized (rejected) youth tend to affiliate disproportionately with each other.
3. Changes in antisocial behavior are proportional to the level of antisocial behavior of one's direct peers.

In this model, antisocial behavior and social status enter as both cause and effect; thus, the model has "endogenous dynamics" (Butner, Amazeen, & Mulvey, 2005), that is, change in system properties over time in the absence of external forces. Together, the above hypotheses posit that early antisocial behavior affects peer affiliations and those affiliations subsequently affect antisocial behavior, further influencing peer affiliations, and so on.

SIENA Models of Social Ecologies

We may represent friendship linkages at any time as a social network (Wasserman & Faust, 1994). To capture change, we imagine a series of *snapshots* representing the state of each possible friendship tie at each point. Conceptual and analytical problems posed by time series of social networks are immediately apparent in, for example, the sheer number of possible ties. In a typical U.S. middle school of 300 students, some 90,000 relationships are possible (counting ties in both directions). Modeling their collective change over time is the rather daunting primary objective of longitudinal network analysis.

In contrast to typical statistical modeling, SIENA takes a decision-simulation approach by randomly choosing network members in simulated continuous time. After an actor's selection, the actor may choose to change a network tie, adding a new link or deleting an existing one. The probability of making a specific choice depends on a set of user-specified effects. Many effects are possible, as discussed below. The decision process may further include simulated choices to change a particular behavior, and behavioral decisions may be effect-driven. Each effect has a parameter associated with it, the size and sign of which determine the effect's magnitude and direction. Statistically sophisticated readers will recognize the decision simulation as a Markov process; hence, Monte-Carlo (MCMC) procedures can provide parameter estimates. Each run takes parameter values from the last one, incrementally changing them to fit the data better until further changes to parameter values do not materially improve model fit. SIENA supports several fit criteria, but we used Method Of Moments because of its superior execution speed. Iterative procedures also provide estimated standard errors (Snijders, 2001, 2005; Snijders et al., 2007).

SIENA allows three types of predictors of link changes. The first is structural, such as out-degrees (unidirectional ties), reciprocity (2-way ties), transitivity (3-way link closure), among others (Wasserman & Faust, 1994). The second comprises measured properties of *edges* or pairs of individuals in the network, such as geographical distance between individuals or membership in one organization. Finally, characteristics of individuals themselves may serve as predictors of link change. These different classes of predictors can interact. The result is a model of tie formation and dissolution probability. We interpret the model much like an ordinary regression model with main and interaction effects. Significance of individual effects are obtained with t-ratios.

SIENA also models change in user-specified characteristics (usually a behavior) hypothesized to depend on aspects of an actor's network embedding (number of direct or reciprocated linkages, the average behavior of those linkages, and others; Snijders et al., 2007). This way, the SIENA-based actor decision model reflects a mutual relationship between behavior and social relationships posited by the rejection confluence idea, that is, they affect each other over time.

Sample and Methods

Subjects. Subjects were 1,289 public middle-school students from eight schools in one district in suburban Oregon. The final sample represents 74 percent recruitment, with 82 percent completing all three waves of assessment, conducted during the fall of sixth, seventh, and eighth grades. The sample was 45 percent male, 55 percent female, primarily European American (79 percent), and with a small percentage of Latino students (4.5 percent), representative of the study community. The final recruitment rate by wave and school varied from 58 to 81 percent, with an unweighted mean of 70 percent. Further procedural details are available elsewhere (Stormshak, Dishion, Light, & Yasui, 2005).

Measures

Social Networks. We defined the networks based on friendship nominations. Upon request, students named three best friends from a class list. We treated a nomination as a direct tie, one that another student may or may not reciprocate.

We performed analyses on *directed* (asymmetrical) network data, using twenty-four adjacency matrices to represent the peer networks of our respondents over time. For each school k = 1, . . . , 8 and each wave t = 1, 2, 3 (corresponding to sixth through eighth grades), nominations were converted to asymmetric n_{kt} (number of students per class) $\times$ n_{kt} matrices, with the (i,j)th entry = 1 if individual i nominated individual j on the relationship criterion, and 0 otherwise. Table 6.1 shows the wave-specific numbers for each school.

Rejection (Social Status). Students also nominated those individuals in their grade as those "with whom you would not like to be in a group." We took the total number of such nominations as a proportion ($\times$ 100, rounded to the nearest integer, a requirement for fitting SIENA models) of the total number in the network (total participants) as a rejection score for each individual.

Antisocial Behavior. The Oregon Healthy Teens Survey (Biglan, Metzler, & Ary, 1994) provided a measure of problem behavior. We used the Antisocial Behavior scale for these analyses (alpha = 0.84), including self-reports of lying, stealing, vandalism, violence, and others. Respondents reply on a 0–5 scale ("never" to "more than 20 times").

Model Testing Protocol. SIENA models normally include standard network structure effects: outdegree, reciprocity, and some form of transitivity. Outdegree is the number of individuals the respondent selects as a friend. Reciprocity is the tendency for individuals to extend more ties if they are reciprocated (that is, if individual j also selects individual i). Transitivity involves "closure" of triads in the network over time; if A links with B and B links with C, then more likely C will eventually link with A. Several specific network statistics reflect transitivity (see Snijders, 2005). We found that "actors at distance 2" (D2) was the most reliable triad closure effect (the fewer such structures there are, the more likely it is that an A-B-C linkage

Table 6.1. Descriptive Statistics for School Networks

School	Wave	Network Size Subjects	Network Total Grade	Percentage	Antisocial Behavior Mean(SD)	Antisocial Behavior Maximum	# More Antisocial Behavior[1] (t – 1)→t	# Less Antisocial Behavior[1] (t – 1)→t
1	1	111	182	61	.15(.27)	2.0	—	—
	2	119	196	61	.20(.39)	2.3	21	14
	3	119	190	63	.32(.35)	1.9	51	10
2	1	94	144	62	.14(.35)	2.6	—	—
	2	104	143	73	.19(.40)	2.1	17	10
	3	101	157	64	.34(.44)	2.4	50	39
3	1	123	171	72	.17(.41)	2.4	—	—
	2	132	192	69	.23(.39)	1.1	26	10
	3	135	192	70	.48(.59)	3.0	64	11
4	1	115	182	63	.24(.50)	3.3	—	—
	2	113	173	65	.26(.39)	1.8	25	19
	3	137	180	76	.43(.39)	2.1	57	17
5	1	131	167	78	.21(.39)	2.3	—	—
	2	133	164	81	.30(.50)	1.8	31	22
	3	121	156	78	.58(.52)	3.7	77	8
6	1	149	103	73	.16(.38)	2.3	—	—
	2	145	106	70	.13(.24)	1.1	14	17
	3	153	204	75	.40(.43)	1.7	70	8
7	1	200	253	79	.11(.26)	2.1	—	—
	2	198	247	80	.14(.30)	1.8	36	19
	3	195	253	77	.41(.50)	3.9	101	10
8	1	85	146	58	.17(.28)	1.3	—	—
	2	116	161	72	.20(.40)	2.2	14	11
	3	107	155	69	.40(.51)	3.3	54	7

[1]Number of individuals increasing or decreasing their antisocial behavior between pairs of waves.
[2]Scale range 0–5.

chain has "closed" through the addition of an A-C link, or the chain itself has disintegrated; hence D2 is essentially an inverse-transitive structure). In some analyses, network structure effects are substantively important, but here they were simply control covariates, included in all models reported below, along with gender.

Testing Confluence. Using SIENA, we estimated separate models for each of the eight schools, based on our experience that school social ecologies may have unique dynamics (Stormshak et al., 1999). We examined three confluence-based hypotheses. With three waves of data, we estimated lag-one effects pooled across the two consecutive two-year periods (grades 6 through 7 and grades 7 through 8). Two of these hypotheses pertain to friendship formation and dissolution (selection): (1) antisocial youth tend to face rejection by their peers, and (2) rejected youth tend to affiliate with each other. To test for these statistical patterns, we included two model effects: Antisocial Behavior Alter (AB-Alter) and Rejection Similarity (Rej Sim). We hypothesized friendship ties were less likely when the Alter had higher levels of antisocial behavior; therefore, we expected this effect to be negative. In contrast, we expected the Rej Sim to be positive; individuals are more likely to form ties with others of similar rejection status. The third hypothesis predicted a positive association between a student's antisocial behavior at time t and that of nominated friends at time $t - 1$ (influence).

Results

Table 6.1 shows mean antisocial scores by school and wave that increase generally from sixth through eighth grades. The increase from seventh to eighth grade is greater than from sixth to seventh. There are obviously differences in average antisocial behavior between schools (largest in school 5, smallest in school 7).

Table 6.1 also shows changes in antisocial behavior between the two pairs of waves. A substantial percentage (about 25 to 50 percent) report behavior changes between waves, with most increasing rather than decreasing. Such change is common in early adolescence. Overall, about 1 to 1.5 percent of ties change between waves, the low percentage reflecting mainly the (typical) sparseness of friendship networks. As a network of 150 individuals includes over 20,000 possible one-way linkages, there are hundreds of link changes evident in the data across each pair of waves. Our models were designed to account for these changes.

Table 6.2 presents final SIENA models estimated for each of the eight schools. All models included four basic structural effects: outdegree, reciprocity, distance-2, and gender similarity (rate effects were modeled but are not presented). For the purpose of this study, we treated these effects as nuisance variables, included to ensure confluence-related effects were not confounded with other well-known influences on friendship tie formation. Table 6.2 shows nearly all these effects to be statistically significant for all

Table 6.2. SIENA Model Results for "3 Best Friend" Linkages

Effects	School 1	School 2	School 3	School 4	School 5	School 6	School 7	School 8
Tie formation covariates								
Outdegree	−2.4*(0.2)	−2.0*(0.1)	−2.0*(0.2)	−1.6*(0.2)	−1.9*(0.1)	−2.3*(0.6)	−1.7*(0.3)	−1.9*(0.3)
Reciprocity	2.4*(0.2)	2.3*(0.1)	2.4*(0.1)	2.7*(0.1)	2.9*(0.2)	2.7*(0.5)	2.6*(0.3)	2.2*(0.4)
Distance 2	−0.6*(0.1)	−0.6*(0.1)	−1.0*(0.1)	−1.2*(0.2)	−1.4*(0.3)	−0.9(0.5)	−1.1*(0.1)	−1.3*(0.4)
Sex similarity	1.1*(0.3)	0.9*(0.1)	1.1*(0.3)	0.6*(0.1)	0.6*(0.2)	0.9(0.5)	0.9*(0.2)	1.1*(0.5)
Tie formation confluence								
AB alter[a]	0.06(0.06)	0.05(0.06)	−0.13*(0.06)	0.01(0.05)	0.34*(0.07)	0.09(0.09)	−0.21(0.20)	−0.29*(0.1)
Rejection[b] similarity	0.6*(0.3)	0.8*(0.3)	1.3*(0.3)	0.6(0.7)	1.4*(0.4)	0.8*(0.3)	1.6(1.0)	0.7(0.6)
AB average alter[c]	1.0(0.6)	0.1(0.4)	0.2(0.3)	−0.1(0.6)	−0.2(0.5)	0.8(0.5)	1.3*(0.5)	0.3(0.7)

Note: Parameter estimates can be interpreted like coefficients in a multinomial logit regression, reflecting the increase (+) or decrease (−) in log-odds of a tie forming for the link-formation part of the model (all effects but the last) and of a one-unit increase (decrease) in antisocial behavior for the behavior part of the model (the AB Average Alter effect only).

[a]If (+), implies ties are more likely to form with more antisocial alters; if (−), they are less likely to form.

[b]If (+), ties are more likely to form between individuals who have a similar level of rejection; if (−), similar rejection implies ties are less likely to form.

[c]If (+), an individual tends to increase his or her level of antisocial behavior at time t + 1 the more antisocial his direct-connect alters were at time t; if (−), the tendency is to decrease such behavior the more antisocial one's direct connect alters.

schools. Outdegree was typically negative and slightly smaller in absolute value than reciprocity; together these parameters suggest that reciprocated (but not asymmetric) ties are likely to form at a rate slightly higher than chance. The negative distance-2 effects indicate a tendency towards "network closure" for ties to link back on themselves to form cycles. Finally, the well-known preference for same-gender friends among early adolescents is reflected in the generally significant "sex similarity" effects; only one school was found to have a nonsignificant gender effect, and in that school it was trend-significant ($p < .10$).

The last three rows of Table 6.2 address confluence hypotheses 1, 2, and 3. Hypothesis 1 stated that antisocial youth should be socially marginalized, which we tested by including an effect of AB-alter in each model. This parameter should be significant and negative if hypothesis 1 is correct. In schools 3 and 8, we see this confirmed, but effects are nonsignificant in 1, 2, 4, 6, and 7. In school 5, the effect is significant but positive: ties are more likely to extend to the antisocial youth. This is clearly the opposite of hypothesis 1 but consistent with other findings related to ecological variation in how antisocial youth affiliate with peers (for example, Stormshak et al., 1999).

Hypothesis 2 implies that rejected youth (often nominated as *disliked*) tend to affiliate disproportionately with each other. A significant rejection confluence effect appears in five schools, with positive trends in the other three, providing compelling support for rejection confluence in that students form into subgroups based on similar experiences with respect to marginalization within their schools.

Finally, hypothesis 3 states that youth who affiliate with more AB-alters will tend to have higher antisocial behavior scores in the next wave. However, the effect appeared in only school 7.

Discussion

The confluence model proposes that rejection by peers influences peer networks by means of high risk youth aggregating into cliques, which then later influences the development of antisocial behavior, especially in adolescence. This simple hypothesis has been difficult to test comprehensively, largely because of the complex methodological issues inherent in analyzing changing networks over time.

The agent-oriented SIENA modeling approach, however, provided a natural framework for such a test. In our analyses, we examined each school as its own ecology. We found universal support for the hypothesis that rejected children tend to affiliate over time. Antisocial youth, however, were not always peer rejected. Consistent with the findings of others, in some schools, antisocial behavior was associated with acceptance and even popularity (for example, Rodkin et al., 2000; Rodkin, Farmer, Pearl, & Van Acker, 2006). Finally, we found evidence that antisocial affiliation predicted subsequent growth in antisocial behavior—that is, influence—in only one middle school.

Clearly it was useful to analyze each school separately, as it seems that each school presents with unique network dynamics. From a substantive perspective, it is evident that the confluence hypothesis can only account for peer-level antisocial homophily and the growth of antisocial behavior over time in one of these eight schools. What is to be made of these results?

We suggest three potentially productive directions for future research. First, of course it may turn out that the endogenous growth of antisocial behavior is relatively rare, occurring only under certain special conditions. If true, this would not be uninteresting—hundreds or thousands of middle schools nationwide may be unwittingly structured to allow this type of pathological process. Therefore, one fruitful approach is to study antisocial peer processes within and across specific school ecologies. Multilevel designs can potentially disentangle school-level effects (neighborhood, composition, administrative procedures) versus cohort composition effects, either or both of which might account for this variation. For example, we might find that schools with low overall levels of peer rejection confluence also exhibit less peer influence on antisocial behavior. Perhaps in those ecologies, the only sources of growth in such behavior are exogenous.

Second, given ancillary evidence of the ubiquity of social influence among adolescents, it is altogether possible that to detect such effects in natural settings, much better data are required. Frequent assessments of peer relationships and behaviors are required to accurately observe which changes seem to be causes (having occurred earlier in time) and which are effects (having occurred later). As the interval between observations increases, more of these events will appear to be "ties," that is, both occurring in the same time period. Ties are useless as evidence for whether affiliation caused behavior (influence) or behavior caused affiliation (selection). The yearly assessment strategy used in this study may be inadequate to the task. The same point may apply to other network-based studies that found weak or absent influence effects (see Engels, Vitaro, Den Exter Blokland, de Kemp, & Scholt, 2004; Ennett & Bauman, 1994; Jaccard, Blanton, & Dodge, 2005).

Third, we suggest that social networking research be linked at some point with direct observation research. We know from direct observation studies that deviancy training as observed with a "friend" at age thirteen predicts growth in multiple forms of problem behavior well into adulthood (for example, Dishion, Nelson, Winter & Bullock, 2004). Often youth identified as friends are not part of the school environment or even especially close. Rather, they are more nearly "regular associates," peers with whom the child spends a great deal of time. Thus, some peer environments may promote influence, but not necessarily from friendships as defined in previous studies. Adapting the types of observational methods used with smaller groups of high-risk children (for example, Dishion, Poulin, & Burraston, 2001) to larger peer social ecologies could help identify some of these mechanisms and the contexts in which they arise.

Nevertheless, even if only some school social ecologies unwittingly promote the growth of antisocial behavior or other behavior problems, it is important to continue to develop our research methods to help engineer less contagion-prone environments. Every teacher and principal knows that cohorts of students can vary dramatically in their levels of problem behavior even within one school. Giving adults better tools to manage peer environments would help students with learning and character development and school staff with teaching environment and stress. Festinger, Schachter, and Back (1950) found that relationships between individuals are less likely when the opportunity for chance encounters is lower; systematically separating at-risk youth (contrary to much current practice) or lessening their opportunities for unsupervised interaction provide possible examples. Nevertheless, we must be able to reliably predict the absence and the presence of key dynamics before this strategy can be reliably implemented, underscoring the critical importance of more powerful research designs.

References

Bauman, K. E., & Fisher, L. A. (1986). On the measurement of friend behavior in research on friend influence and selection: Findings from longitudinal studies of adolescent smoking and drinking. *Journal of Youth and Adolescence, 15*, 345–53.

Biglan, A., Metzler, C. W., & Ary, D. V. (1994). Increasing the prevalence of successful children: The case for community intervention research. *Behavior Analyst, 17*, 335–51.

Butner, J., Amazeen, P. G., & Mulvey, G. M. (2005). Multilevel modeling of two cyclical processes: Extending differential structural equation modeling to nonlinear coupled systems. *Psychological Methods, 10*(2), 159–177.

Cairns, R. B., Neckerman, H. J., & Cairns, B. D. (1989). Social networks and the shadows of synchrony. In G. P. Adams, R. Montemayor, & T. P. Gullotta (Eds.), *Biology of adolescent behavior and development* (pp. 275–303). Thousand Oaks, CA: Sage.

Coie, J. D., & Kupersmidt, J. B. (1983). A behavioral analysis of emerging social status in boys groups. *Child Development, 54*, 1400–1416.

Dishion, T. J., Nelson, S. E., & Kavanagh, K. (2003). The family check-up with high-risk young adolescents: Preventing early-onset substance use by parent monitoring. *Behavior Therapy, 34*, 553–571.

Dishion, T. J., Nelson, S. E., Winter, C., & Bullock, B. M. (2004). Adolescent friendship as a dynamic system: Entropy and deviance in the etiology and course of antisocial behavior. *Journal of Abnormal Child Psychology, 32*, 651–663.

Dishion, T. J., Nelson, S. E., & Yasui, M. (2005). Predicting early adolescent gang involvement from middle school adaptation. *Journal of Clinical Child and Adolescent Psychology, 34*(1), 62–73.

Dishion, T. J., & Patterson, G. R. (2006). The development and ecology of antisocial behavior. In D. Cicchetti & D. J. Cohen (Eds.), *Developmental psychopathology. Vol. 3: Risk, disorder, and adaptation* (pp. 503–541). Hoboken, NJ: Wiley.

Dishion, T. J., Patterson, G. R., & Griesler, P. C. (1994). Peer adaptations in the development of antisocial behavior: A confluence model. In L. R. Huesmann (Ed.), *Aggressive behavior: Current perspectives* (pp. 61–95). New York: Plenum.

Dishion, T. J., Poulin, F., & Burraston, B. (2001). Peer group dynamics associated with iatrogenic effects in group interventions with high-risk youth (pp. 79–92). In C. Erdly

& D. W. Nangle (Eds.), *Damon's new directions in child development: The role of friendship in psychological adjustment*. San Francisco: Jossey-Bass.

Dodge, K. A. (1983). Behavioral antecedents: A peer social status. *Child Development, 54,* 1386–1399.

Dodge, K. A, Lansford, J. E., Burks, V. S., Bates, J. E., Pettit, G. S., Fontaine, R., et al. (2003). Peer rejection and social information-processing factors in the development of aggressive behavior problems in children. *Child Development, 74*(2), 374–393.

Elliott, D., Huizinga, D., & Ageton, S. S. (1985). *Explaining delinquency and drug use.* Thousand Oaks, CA: Sage.

Engels, R.C.M., Vitaro, F., Den Exter Blokland, E., de Kemp, R., & Scholt, R.H.J. (2004). Influence and selection processes in friendships and adolescent smoking behaviour: The role of parental smoking. *Journal of Adolescence, 27,* 531–44.

Ennett, S. T., & Bauman, K. E. (1994). The contribution of influence and selection to adolescent peer group homogeneity: The case of adolescent cigarette smoking. *Journal of Personality and Social Psychology, 67*(4), 652–663.

Farmer, T. W., & Hollowell, J. H. (1994). Social networks in mainstream classrooms: Social affiliations and behavioral characteristics of students with EBD. *Journal of Emotional and Behavioral Disorders, 2,* 143–156.

Farmer, T. W., Van Acker, R. M., Pearl, R., & Rodkin, P. C. (1999). Social networks and peer-assessed problem behavior in elementary classrooms. *Remedial and Special Education, 20*(4), 244–256.

Festinger, L., Schachter, S., & Back, K. (1950). *Social pressures in informal groups: A study of human factors in housing.* New York: HarperCollins.

Gifford-Smith, M., Dodge, K. A., Dishion, T. J., & McCord, J. (2005). Peer influence in children and adolescents: Crossing the bridge from developmental to intervention science. *Journal of Abnormal Child Psychology, 33*(3), 255–265.

Gold, M. (1970). *Delinquent behavior in an American city.* San Francisco: Brooks & Coleman.

Hartup, W. W. (1992). Friendships and their developmental significance. In H. McGurk (Ed.), *Childhood social development: Contemporary perspectives* (pp. 175–205). Mahwah, NJ: Erlbaum.

Jaccard, J., Blanton, H., & Dodge, T. (2005). Peer influences on risk behavior: An analysis of the effects of a close friend. *Developmental Psychology, 41*(1), 135–147.

Kenny, D. A., & Judd, C. M. (1986). Consequences of violating the independence assumption in analysis of variance. *Psychological Bulletin, 99,* 422–431.

Kessler, R. C., & Greenberg, D. F. (1981). *Linear panel analysis: Models of quantitative change.* Orlando, FL: Academic Press.

Marsden, P. V. (2005). Recent developments in network measurement. In P. J. Carrington, J. Scott, & S. Wasserman (Eds.), *Models and methods in social network analysis* (pp. 8–30). Cambridge: Cambridge University Press.

Murray, D. M., & Hannan, P. J. (1990). Planning for the appropriate analysis in school-based drug use prevention studies. *Journal of Consulting and Clinical Psychology, 58*(4), 458–468.

Olson, S. L. (1992). Development of conduct problems and peer rejection in pre-school children: A social systems analysis. *Journal of Abnormal Child Psychology, 20,* 327–350.

Prinstein, M. J., & Wang, S. S. (2007). False consensus and adolescent peer contagion: Examining discrepancies between perceptions and actual reported levels of friends' deviant and health risk behaviors. *Journal of Abnormal Child Psychology, 33*(3), 293–306.

Rodkin, P. C., Farmer, T. W., Pearl, R., & Van Acker, R. M. (2000). Heterogeneity of popular boys: Antisocial and prosocial configurations. *Developmental Psychology, 36,* 14–24.

Rodkin, P. C., Farmer, T. W., Pearl, R., & Van Acker, R. M. (2006). They're cool: Social status and peer group supports for aggressive boys and girls. *Social Development, 15*(2), 175–204.

Snijders, T.A.B. (2001). The statistical evaluation of social network dynamics. In M. E. Sobel & M. P. Becker (Eds.), *Sociological methodology*. Boston: Basil Blackwell.

Snijders, T.A.B. (2005). Models for longitudinal network data. In P. J. Carrington, J. Scott, & S. Wasserman (Eds.), *Models and methods in social network analysis* (pp. 215–247). Cambridge: Cambridge University Press.

Snijders, T.A.B., Steglich, C.E.G., & Schweinberger, M. (2006). Modeling the coevolution of networks and behavior. In K. van Montfort, H. Oud, & A. Satorra (Eds.), *Longitudinal models in the behavioral and related sciences*. Mahwah, NJ: Erlbaum.

Snijders, T.A.B., Steglich, C.E.G., Schweinberger, M., & Huisman, M. (2007). *Manual for SIENA version 3*. Gröningen, The Netherlands: University of Gröningen, ICS, Department of Sociology.

Stormshak, E. A., Dishion, T. J., Light, J., & Yasui, M. (2005). Implementing family-centered interventions within the public middle school: Linking service delivery to change in problem behavior. *Journal of Abnormal Child Psychology, 33,* 723–33.

Stormshak, E. A., Bierman, K. L., Bruschi, C., Dodge, K. A., Coie, J., & the Conduct Problems Research Group (1999). The relation between behavior problems and peer preference in different classroom contexts. *Child Development, 70*(1), 169–182.

Wasserman, S., & Faust, K. (1994). *Social network analysis: Methods and applications.* Cambridge: Cambridge University Press.

JOHN M. LIGHT *is associate scientist at the Oregon Research Institute.*

THOMAS J. DISHION *is professor of psychology and school psychology and the director of the Child and Family Center at the University of Oregon.*

Much of children's interactions with peers take place in cliques or small groups that they themselves form. What happens in these groups has important effects on children's further social and academic development. The chapters in this volume present the most recent ideas and methods to study childhood cliques and groups.

7

New Perspectives on Social Networks in the Study of Peer Relations

Antonius H. N. Cillessen

Individuals, Dyads, and Groups

Social developmentalists typically distinguish three levels of analysis in the study of peer relations in childhood and adolescence: individual, dyadic, and group (Rubin, Bukowski, & Parker, 2006). At the individual level of analysis, sociometric status and individual social behavior are studied. At the dyadic level, researchers traditionally study friendships but increasingly also other types of relationships such as enemies, mutually aggressive dyads, bully-victim pairs, and romantic relationships. The objects of study at the group level of analysis are the social networks, groups, and cliques to which children and adolescents belong. The phenomena at each of these three levels are uniquely affected by and have unique effects on social development (Rubin et al., 2006). Although the importance of all three levels for our understanding of the developmental significance of peer relations has been recognized, there is relatively more research at the individual and dyadic levels of analysis than at the group level. The chapters in this volume correct this trend. They make significant contributions to the study of peer relations at the group level through detailed examinations of children's social networks. Below, I will first discuss some of the reasons why peer relations researchers may have studied social networks less frequently than individuals and dyads and how the chapters of this volume counteract this trend. In addition, the contributions to this volume exemplify several developments

in peer relations research. I will also outline these recent developments and demonstrate how the chapters reflect them.

Challenges in the Developmental Study of Social Networks

Several studies have identified the structural features of social networks in childhood and adolescence and considered the effects of social network membership on various outcomes (for example, Brown & Lohr, 1987; Cairns, Cairns, Neckerman, Gest, & Gariépy, 1988; Kindermann, 1996; Urberg, Degirmencioglu, & Pilgrim, 1997). This research has shown that social networks are an important context for socialization of desirable as well as undesirable developmental outcomes. Social networks play a role in the development of antisocial behavior and delinquency, as well as academic and mental health outcomes (Dishion, McCord, & Poulin, 1999; Espelage, Holt, & Henkel, 2003). Given the developmental importance of social networks, it is surprising that they have been studied less often than individual peer status and dyadic relationships.

Why have social networks been studied less frequently than individuals and dyads? One reason is that social networks are more difficult to define and operationalize. Most researchers agree that peer status refers to a within-group rank ordering of individuals according to their degree of acceptance, rejection, popularity, or dominance. There is also consensus about how to classify children into sociometric status types or categories (Cillessen & Bukowski, 2000). The measurement of dyadic relationships is relatively straightforward as well. Friendships are typically derived from reciprocal best friend nominations, whereas unilateral friend nominations do not count as true friendships. Similarly, operational definitions have been used to identify enemies (Hodges & Card, 2003) or mutually aggressive pairs (Coie et al., 1999). It would be misleading to suggest that all methodological problems in the measurement of individual and dyadic characteristics have been solved, and these methods continue to evolve. Yet, it is generally quite clear how to conceptualize and measure peer relations at these levels.

The identification of social networks is typically more complex and challenging than the determination of sociometric status or a friendship relationship. Social networks are not fixed entities but clusters of connected individuals that change over time. At any given time, the members of a network are in it with varying degrees of centrality. Over time, the centrality of a network member may increase or decrease. At the periphery, the boundaries of the network are relatively open—individuals move in and out of the group. These characteristics make it harder to judge whether at any given time a person is or is not a group member. A related complication is that most individuals belong to more than one group at the same time, whereas the researcher may prefer to assign each person to exactly one group. Finally, the parameters that characterize social networks vary with development. For example, networks may be more unstable at certain ages than at others. These developmental changes also make it harder to uniformly conceptualize and operationally define social networks.

In addition to the conceptual complexity, social networks may have been studied less frequently than individuals or dyads because the methodologies for assessing social networks tend to be labor intensive and complex, both in data collection and data manipulation. The chapters in this volume illustrate this. At the data collection stage, some take simple friendship peer nominations as input, whereas others require individual interviews or observations. Social networks researchers are interested in categorical information (what the groups are and who is in them) and continuous information at the individual (for example, centrality) and group levels (for example, cohesiveness). Whatever the collection method, the derivation of this information requires complex quantification of the data. Finally, although traditional statistical methods can handle individual data, and great progress has been made in the statistical analysis of dyadic data (see Kenny, Kashy, & Cook, 2006), similar guidelines are not yet available for the analysis of network data in the developmental literature.

Taken together, these characteristics make the study of social networks more difficult but not less important. Collectively, the chapters in this volume present elegant and intelligent solutions to these challenges. They present sound definitions of social networks that do justice to their complexity and dynamic nature, detailed measurement and scoring techniques, and sophisticated statistical methods. Thus, the chapters in this volume provide avenues to increase the frequency of research on children's social networks and set the standards to do so.

Social Networks as an Opportunity for Integration

Peer relations researchers have maintained a fairly strict division between individuals, dyads, and groups. In reality, this distinction is less strong than this conceptual framework suggests. A sharp distinction between the levels does not do full justice to the complex nesting of peer relations and the dynamic changes that take place over time within and across school years. Individual status, dyadic relationships, and social networks are multiple layers of the social context of peer relations that are weighted differently across development. Although it is a useful heuristic, we have to ask whether a strict distinction between individuals, dyads, and groups is still sufficient to describe the complex structure of peer relations. At a minimum, we need a method to tie them together. Individuals are in dyads, dyads are nested in groups, and individuals are part of multiple dyads and groups that may be unique or may overlap. This complex nesting of relationships is fluid over time and changes developmentally. We face the task of finding a new language that does justice to this complex structure.

The chapters of this volume provide important steps in this direction by showing how social networks can be studied while also taking individuals and dyads into account. Light and Dishion (this volume) examined the connection between social network involvement, individual antisocial behavior, and the formation of best friend ties. Espelage, Green, and Wasserman (this volume) examined the aggregation of individual attitudes toward bullying within clique structures that were derived from friendship ties. Hanish et al. (this volume) followed the reverse path by showing how parameters derived from network analysis can be used as individual level parameters that can be analyzed with traditional multivariate methods. Gest, Davidson, Rulison, Moody, and Welsh and Rodkin, Wilson, and Ahn (both this volume) examined the role of individual gender and ethnicity in social networks. Together, these chapters demonstrate that understanding social networks implies the examination of individual and dyadic variables. Hence, the study of social networks does justice to the complex multilevel nature of peer groups, rather than treating individuals, dyads, and groups as separate entities.

New Trends in the Study of Peer Relations

Four new trends can be observed that characterize the development of peer relations research in recent years. Each of these trends is also present in the chapters in this volume.

First, the methods for the study of peer relations have been expanded substantially. When research on peer relations gained prominence in the 1980s, it was dominated by an interest in either one of two methods: sociometric status or friendship dyads. Within these areas, methods have been expanded in various directions. But most importantly, the study of social networks has grown substantially, using increasingly sophisticated methods. The chapters in this volume attest to this development. The authors used state of the art methods including SIENA (Light & Dishion, this volume), p* (Espelage et al., this volume), SCM (Gest, et al., this volume), the Q-connectivity method (Hanish et al., this issue), and new indices for the analysis of ethnic diversity (Rodkin et al., this volume). Thus, each chapter contributes to the further growth of social network methods for peer relations research.

Second, as methods have expanded, the field of peer relations research has also become more multidisciplinary. There is a long tradition of studying social networks in sociology. Although this tradition has long existed parallel with, but separate from the developmental literature, the sociological and developmental approaches are now increasingly integrated. The researchers in this volume use methods from developmental psychology, sociology of education, mathematical sociology, and mathematical statistics while also making connections to the field of developmental criminology.

Thus, the chapters in this volume also evidence the growing interdisciplinary nature of research on peer relations.

Third, the field of peer relations has become more developmental. In the past, researchers often operated under the assumption of developmental invariance. For example, it has sometimes been implicitly assumed that the correlates of sociometric status are equal in all age groups, whereas, in fact, they change over time. Similarly, age changes need to be considered in the study of peer networks, and the current chapters attest to this. The authors show sensitivity to developmental differences in their choice of data collection methods. Hanish and colleagues (this volume) used observations to quantify preschool peer networks, whereas best friend nominations and peer nominations for friendships or affiliation ("who do you hang around with?") were the appropriate methods for assessing middle childhood and adolescent peer networks (Espelage et al., Gest et al., Light & Dishion, and Rodkin et al., all this volume). The authors also show sensitivity to developmental differences in the functions of social networks. Hanish et al. found that preschoolers' group networks were sometimes unstable perhaps because they may serve exploratory social functions at this age group. Yet at all age groups, social networks may be important to early academic skills (Hanish et al.), children's emerging understanding of gender (Gest et al.) and ethnicity (Rodkin et al.), and the emergence or prevention of bullying (Espelage et al.) and antisocial behaviors (Light & Dishion).

Fourth, as the field has become more developmental it has also become more dynamic. Although dynamic systems theory has a long history in developmental psychology (for example, Miller, 2002), the applications have been primarily in the fields of cognitive and motor development (see, for example, Thelen & Smith, 1998). Applications of dynamic systems theory to social development are only recently emerging (for example, Granic & Dishion, 2003; Granic & Patterson, 2006). The chapters in this volume contribute to this trend by conceptualizing social networks as fluid entities that change dynamically over time and by showing which parameters derived from social network assessments can be used for dynamic systems analyses (for example, Hanish et al., and Light & Dishion, both this volume).

New Perspectives on Social Networks

As indicated, the chapters in this volume exemplify these new trends. They show an expansion of methods (for example, SIENA, p*), a multidisciplinary perspective (crossing the boundaries of developmental psychology, sociology, criminology, and mathematical statistics), and increasingly developmental and dynamic perspectives. Thus, they evidence the trends that characterize peer relations research today.

Light and Dishion (this volume) applied the principles of dynamic systems to the study of social networks using SIENA (Snijders, Steglich,

Schweinberger, & Huisman, 2007). They found effects of both development (increases in network antisociality) and context (school differences). Their study illustrates the increasing multidisciplinarity of peer relations research by answering questions from developmental criminology using methods from mathematical sociology. This chapter also illustrates the integrated perspective on the study of peers: although dyads were the building blocks for the construction of networks, parameters derived from the network structure such as outdegree, reciprocity, and rejection similarity were assigned to individuals for individual level analyses. Thus, this chapter shows the interconnections between individual, dyadic, and network level information in a dynamic and developmental perspective.

Espelage et al. (this volume) examined structural questions of social networks related to bullying. This chapter makes a strong connection to theory and derives rival predictions from differing theories of peer influence. The chapter specifically highlights the role of group norms toward bullying. Studies have shown that the correlates of peer acceptance and rejection vary depending on group norms in artificially constructed aggregates such as contrived play groups (Boivin, Dodge, & Coie, 1995), classrooms (Stormshak, Bierman, Brushi, Dodge, & Coie, 1999), or intervention groups (Wright, Giammarino, & Parad, 1986). Espelage et al. show that the same applies to naturally occurring social networks. Finally, this chapter makes an important connection between the structural characteristics of groups and processes of peer influence. Espelage et al. show explicitly how peer influence may be linked to the structural characteristics of networks.

The work by Hanish and colleagues (this volume) illustrates the dynamic systems view of social networks. As indicated, the dynamic conceptualizing of peer relations is an important agenda for future research. This chapter does exactly that. It uses advanced methods to examine the unfolding of interactions in groups over time. The next step in this research will be to examine which individual or contextual parameters steer the system in a certain direction. As in Light and Dishion's chapter, Hanish et al. demonstrate that social networks cannot be thought of as static and that the most important insights into the role of social networks will come from over-time data. Developmental time can then be taken into account as well. A noteworthy finding of this study is the relative instability of the social networks of young children. A possible reason for this finding is that social networks may serve a different developmental function in this age group than in older age groups when they are more stable according to other methods. This leads to the interesting question of what the Q-connectivity parameters would be if they are assessed in older age groups.

Gest and colleagues (this volume) focused on the role of gender in the organization of children's social networks. Their chapter explored similarities and differences in boys' and girls' social networks, specifically social cohesiveness and centralization. The chapter addressed the important question of whether the social networks of boys and girls are equally cohesive and have equal status distributions. An important starting point of this chapter is the frequently made assumption that girls are more dyad-focused whereas boys are more group-focused. Previous studies from different research traditions have shown mixed findings in this respect. An interesting finding in this chapter is the relative lack of gender differences in the structural aspects of social networks for the specific age group of this study. As the authors conclude, gender differences in the characteristics of peer affiliations may sometimes have been overestimated, and social networks may be more similar than different by gender. It should be recognized, however, that this relative lack of differences was found after the networks had been identified on the basis of friendship choices. This leaves open the possibility that boys and girls use their own gender-specific definitions of friendship when they generate these choices. Thus, substantive differences in the foundation of the networks may still exist—for example, boys and girls may have used different criteria when they identified a peer as a friend.

There is also an interesting analogy between these findings and those of Rodkin and colleagues (this volume), who found important effects of the ethnic composition of a social network. Gest et al. examined groups that were homogenous by gender, and, in fact, mixed-sex networks were excluded from the analyses. Perhaps more gender differences will be found if mixed groups are analyzed—this may be a promising avenue for future research. In a study with six-year-old children, Green, Cillessen, Berthelsen, Irving, and Catherwood (2003) found that the gender composition of play groups has a strong impact on children's cooperative and competitive behavior. For some variables, a mixed-gender context increased gender differences compared to a same-sex environment. Similarly, gender may have more powerful effects in mixed-sex networks than in same-sex networks. Because the occurrence of mixed-sex networks increases with development, the effects may be further exacerbated in older age groups.

Rodkin and colleagues (this volume) focused on the role of racial diversity in the formation of social networks. Although peer relations researchers have addressed the role of ethnicity at the individual level of analysis (see, for example, Graham, 2006), Rodkin and colleagues are taking this research a step further by examining diversity in social networks. In previous research from our own lab, we have found mixed results regarding the role of ethnicity. In one study (LaFontana & Cillessen, 2007), we examined the peer nominations of fourth through eighth graders in an ethnically mixed low-SES school system in which one-third of the student population was white, one-third African American, and one-third Latino. In this study, we found no evidence for racial bias in the sense that children were equally likely to choose same-race and other-race peers for both positive and negative sociometric criteria. However, in a longitudinal study in a school system in which the student population was two-thirds white and one-third minority (either African American or Latino), students gradually self-selected into racially homogeneous cliques when they were followed from grade 4 to grade 12 (Cillessen & Borch, 2005). Thus, effects of ethnicity varied depending on whether individuals or social networks were the unit of analysis. However, the studies also differed in age groups, ethnic distribution, and study design. More research is needed to disentangle the effects of these various factors.

The study by Rodkin makes an important step in this direction by proposing two new indices to measure classroom ethnic diversity. These indexes were then used in elegant multilevel models. Consistent with the findings by Gest and colleagues, relatively few gender differences were found. Overall, Rodkin et al. presented a pessimistic view on racial bias in children, consistent with our findings of increasing racial segregation of adolescent social networks but inconsistent with our finding of a lack of bias in individual peer nominations. Collectively, these studies emphasize that racial bias is a group level phenomenon, even among children. Racial bias may be an emergent property of groups that is not rooted in the individual. Consequently, the ethnic composition of classrooms, schools, and neighborhoods may have strong implications for the occurrence of racial bias among children. These effects need to be taken into account in the design of classrooms and schools (see Graham, 2006).

Conclusion

Individuals, dyads, and groups are multiple layers of a complex social structure that influence each other reciprocally and change over time. Although this social structure may be relatively stable for adults, it changes quickly in childhood and adolescence due to developmental factors (for example, emergence of friendships in early childhood, growth of peer groups in middle childhood, development of romantic interests in early adolescence) and social structural factors (for example, school transitions). The study of social networks provides an overarching framework for the longitudinal examination of the peer system in childhood and adolescence. The chapters in this volume present the methods and analytic tools that this framework requires.

Two recommendations for future research can be made. First, a methodological program of research is needed to compare the new methods presented in this volume and determine their overlap and distinctions. Second, new substantive research is needed that combines the main research questions of these studies. This research would examine the dynamic change in children's social networks over time, incorporate gender and ethnicity as moderators, include group norms within each network as mediators, and examine important outcomes such as antisocial behavior and academic achievement. This research would integrate individual and dyadic characteristics in the study of social networks to yield a dynamic developmental perspective on the role of peers in the social and academic development of children and youth. The chapters in this volume set the stage for these important research agendas for the next decade of peer relations research.

References

Boivin, M., Dodge, K. A., & Coie, J. D. (1995). Individual-group behavioral similarity and peer status in experimental play groups of boys: The social misfit revisited. *Journal of Personality and Social Psychology, 69,* 269–279.

Brown, B. B., & Lohr, M. J. (1987). Peer-group affiliation and adolescent self-esteem: An integration of ego-identity and symbolic-interaction theories. *Journal of Personality and Social Psychology, 52,* 47–55.

Cairns, R. B., Cairns, B. D., Neckerman, H. J., Gest, S. D., & Gariépy, J. (1988). Social networks and aggressive behavior: Peer support or peer rejection. *Developmental Psychology, 24,* 815–823.

Cillessen, A.H.N., & Borch, C. (2005, April). *Social network centrality and clique membership from grade 4 to grade 12: Results from a 9-year longitudinal study.* Paper presented at the biennial meeting of the Society for Research in Child Development, Atlanta, GA.

Cillessen, A.H.N., & Bukowski, W. M. (Eds.). (2000). *Recent advances in the measurement of acceptance and rejection in the peer system.* San Francisco: Jossey-Bass.

Coie, J. D., Cillessen, A.H.N., Dodge, K. A., Hubbard, J. A., Schwartz, D., Lemerise, E. D., et al. (1999). It takes two to fight: A test of relational factors and a method for assessing aggressive dyads. *Developmental Psychology, 35,* 1179–1188.

Dishion, T. J., McCord, J., & Poulin, F. (1999). When interventions harm: Peer groups and problem behavior. *American Psychologist, 54,* 755–764.

Espelage, D. L., Holt, M. K., & Henkel, R. R. (2003). Examination of peer group contextual effects on aggression during early adolescence. *Child Development, 74,* 205–220.

Graham, S. (2006). Peer victimization in school: Exploring the ethnic context. *Current Directions in Psychological Science, 15,* 317–321.

Granic, I., & Dishion, T. J. (2003). Deviant talk in adolescent friendships: A step toward measuring a pathogenic attractor process. *Social Development, 12,* 314–334.

Granic, I., & Patterson, G. R. (2006). Toward a comprehensive model of antisocial development: A dynamic systems approach. *Psychological Review, 113,* 101–131.

Green, V. A., Cillessen, A.H.N., Berthelsen, D., Irving, K., & Catherwood, D. (2003). The effect of gender context on children's social behavior in a limited resource situation: An observational study. *Social Development, 12,* 586–604.

Hodges, E.V.E., & Card, N. A. (Eds.). (2003). *Enemies and the darker side of peer relations.* San Francisco: Jossey-Bass

Kenny, D. A., Kashy, D. A., & Cook, W. L. (2006). *Dyadic data analysis.* New York: Guilford Press.

Kindermann, T. A. (1996). Strategies for the study of individual development within naturally-existing peer groups. *Social Development, 5,* 158–173.

LaFontana, K. M., & Cillessen, A.H.N. (2007). *Assessing perceiver effects in sociometric data: Stereotyping and accuracy among different ethnic groups.* Unpublished manuscript, Department of Psychology, Sacred Heart University, Fairfield, CT.

Miller, P. H. (2002). *Theories of developmental psychology.* New York: Worth.

Rubin, K. H., Bukowski, W. M., & Parker, J. G. (2006). Peer interactions, relationships, and groups. In W. Damon (Series Ed.) & N. Eisenberg (Vol. Ed.), *Handbook of child psychology (Vol. 3): Social, emotional, and personality development* (6th ed., pp. 571–645). Hoboken, NJ: Wiley.

Snijders, T.A.B., Steglich, C.E.G., Schweinberger, M., & Huisman, M. (2007). *Manual for SIENA version 3.* Universiteit Gröningen, The Netherlands, Department of Sociology.

Stormshak, E. A., Bierman, K. L., Brushi, C., Dodge, K. A., & Coie, J. D. (1999). The relation between behavior problems and peer preference in different classroom contexts. Child Development, 70, 169–182.

Thelen, E., & Smith, L. B. (1998). Dynamic systems theory. In W. Damon (Series Ed.) & R. M. Lerner (Vol. Ed.), *Handbook of child psychology (Vol. 1): Theoretical models of human development* (5th ed., pp. 563–634). Hoboken, NJ: Wiley.

Urberg, K. A., Degirmencioglu, S. M., & Pilgrim, C. (1997). Close friend and group influence on adolescent cigarette smoking and alcohol use. *Developmental Psychology, 33*, 834–844.

Wright, J. C., Giammarino, M., & Parad, H. W. (1986). Social status in small groups: Individual-group similarity and the social "misfit." *Journal of Personality and Social Psychology, 50*, 523–536.

ANTONIUS H. N. CILLESSEN is associate professor of psychology at the University of Connecticut.

8

The methodological and theoretical advances in this volume provide new perspectives on longstanding questions about the extent to which both complementarity and reciprocity underlie social relationships. These chapters highlight innovative approaches for clarifying the role of contextual and developmental variations in social structures and processes that are at the core of developmental social network science.

Studying the Individual Within the Peer Context: Are We on Target?

Thomas W. Farmer

> The emphasis of modern educational theory on the socioemotional aspects of human growth has imposed the necessity of developing techniques for evaluating the degree and character of social development. The problem has been complicated by the fact that social development applies not only to the individual but also to the social organization of which he is a part. Variations occur not only in the social status of a particular person within the group, but also in the structure of the group itself—that is, in the frequency, strength, pattern, and basis of the interrelationships which bind the group together and give it distinctive character.
>
> Urie Bronfenbrenner, 1943

A decade ago, I had the pleasure of spending an afternoon with Dr. Bronfenbrenner and showing him the methods and findings of the research we were conducting on social networks at the Center for Developmental Science. After listening carefully and asking several questions, he commented that our research was important because we were trying to understand the individual within the context of the classroom ecology. But he went on to say that although he was encouraged by our efforts, he was also disappointed

---

This work was supported in part by two grants from the Institute of Education Sciences (R305A040056 and R305030162). The comments here reflect the views of the author and do not represent the funding agency.

because it appeared that the field had not moved very far since his doctoral work in the 1940s. He pointed out that our focus of examining children's social position in distinct peer groups and the position of each group within the hierarchy of all groups in the classroom social structure was not far from the bull's-eye target procedure he had used to study social status in his dissertation.

Dr. Bronfenbrenner went on to elucidate three concerns in social network research that reflect the quote that opens this chapter. First, because social contexts are not simply a product of organizational factors, but reflect characteristics of the individuals of which they are composed, it is tricky business to infer social positions across contexts because the mix of individuals can impact the structural components of groups and the resultant social roles of the children that make up the peer ecology. Second, because the development of children and groups are both dynamic, it is necessary to establish measures and analytic procedures that can capture dynamic change in each in relation to the other. Third, a comprehensive analysis of social development requires not only understanding change in individuals and contexts in relation to each other but also demands the measured investigation of the processes and mechanisms that link each to the other and that promote the dynamic interchanges that guide ontogeny.

In the years following this conversation, I have attempted to keep an eye toward addressing these issues in my own research, but this has been an elusive goal. Thus, as I read the chapters in this volume, I viewed them from the lens of Dr. Bronfenbrenner's comments. Although no one chapter addresses all three concerns outlined above, collectively there is considerable promise in these chapters. On this score, I provide a brief overview of these studies and emphasize their methodological and conceptual contributions. I conclude with a discussion of how this work may help address areas that have not been adequately explored with prior methodologies and theoretical frameworks.

Overview

This is an eclectic group of chapters that use vastly different methodologies, focus on distinct content areas, and examine diverse conceptual issues. Yet, the five studies presented here share a common center as each is aimed at elucidating structural features of social networks and their contributions to development.

Hanish and colleagues (this volume) present the Q-connectivity method as an approach for using observations of peer play interactions to identify social networks of preschoolers. One strength of this methodology is that it uses the individual as the unit of analysis and yields information on the social networks of each child. From this vantage, the data indicate that there are considerable individual differences in the degree to which children interact with the same group, and it appears that many preschoolers become engaged with multiple networks. This suggests that not only must we be careful about conceptualizing social networks as global classroom structures but also consider them as being individually constructed and, in some ways, unique to each member of the broader social unit.

In a similar vein, Espelage and colleagues (this volume) use p* analysis to examine social network structures by starting with and building out from the individual. With this approach, lower-level friendship ties (the dyad and triad) are used to specify more complex network structures. As the authors suggest, these procedures enhance the ability to investigate mechanisms of peer influence and the evolution of peer groups. At a conceptual level, this work indicates that children's social ties reflect a complexity of relations within a network and suggest that peer group effects build from these lower-order relationships. Therefore, investigations of peer influence should not only center on the totality of the group but also consider the focal child's specific ties within the group.

Gest and colleagues (this volume) examined gender differences in group cohesion and status hierarchies in fifth and seventh grades. Social Cognitive Mapping Procedures and principal component analysis were used to identify social networks, and friendship and "liked most" nominations were used to examine *density, reciprocity, distinctiveness,* and *status hierarchy.* Beyond showing that there were many similarities between boys' and girls' groups, this research demonstrated that friendship and liking nominations were much more likely to fall within rather than between groups. Conceptually, this suggests that although friendships and social acceptance are distinct from the peer group, they are highly centralized to the group. Further analyses of the linkages among these variables may help clarify social processes and roles within peer groups.

Rodkin and colleagues (this volume) explore the social integration of African American and European American children in relation to the racial and ethnic composition of the classroom. By using a social segregation index, these researchers examined tendencies toward segregation in relation to whether classrooms were composed primarily of black students, white students, or were racially diverse with no clear majority. In addition to demonstrating differential levels of segregation in relation to classroom composition, an analysis of liked-least nominations indicated a complex relationship between cross-race antipathies and whether classrooms were majority black or white. High levels of segregation among black students in majority white classrooms were accompanied by high cross-race antipathies among white students. Beyond the important contributions to understanding ethnic and racial relations in school, the conceptual framework and analytical approaches used in this study may have broader application for investigating patterns of homophily and intergroup relations in classrooms.

Light and Dishion (this volume) used the SIENA model of social network analysis to examine the confluence model of antisocial behavior. According to this model, antisocial behavior predicts social marginalization, marginalized (rejected) youth tend to affiliate disproportionately with each other, and changes in antisocial behavior are proportional to the level of antisocial behavior of one's direct peers. These researchers conducted analyses at the school level and demonstrated that although components of this model were evident in each of the eight participating schools, the overall results were quite mixed. Specifically, although there was strong support for the expectation that rejected (that is, unpopular) youth tend to associate with each other, antisocial behavior was not associated with peer rejection in 75 percent of the schools. In addition, the view that antisocial peers operate as a behavioral contagion was supported in only one school. The results of this study demonstrate the complexities of the peer relations of aggressive youth and the importance of exploring variability across schools. Conceptually, the findings reported here are consistent with the view that there may be diverse patterns of peer support for antisocial behavior in schools (see also Farmer, Estell, Bishop, O'Neal, & Cairns, 2003; Farmer, Leung, Pearl, Rodkin, Cadwallader, & Van Acker, 2002).

Looking Forward

The overview of the contributions of these chapters highlights the complexities of the methodologies that have been developed to examine ontogeny within the peer system. Although we have made tremendous progress in terms of assessing network structures while maintaining a focus on individual development, it seems there is much work ahead until we are able to fully elucidate processes and mechanisms that link individual adaptation to peer group structures and broader classroom and school social systems. I believe that some of the limitations in this area have grown from methodological and theoretical expediency.

In terms of methodological expediency, many of the measurement models currently used in the social development literature focus on survey data. This allows researchers to efficiently and economically gather extensive data on student, peer, and teacher perspectives of peer acceptance, peer networks, and individual students' social and behavioral characteristics. The payoff to this approach is that large samples and databases can be quickly prepared for analyses and dissemination. Although survey data can be used to infer some social factors and processes, such as cohesiveness, social network centrality, and selective affiliation, other constructs require more extensive measurement approaches. These may include sequential observations across extended periods of time, individual narrative accounts of key social events and incidents, and short-term longitudinal classroom level analyses of key constructs, such as social roles, peer groups, and social structures. Such endeavors are costly in terms of data collection, data preparation, and analyses. Furthermore, these efforts often take considerable time from initiation to publication.

Theoretical expediency is tied to methodological expediency. Some theories link well to parsimonious measurement and analytical approaches. For example, sociometric status measures provide for easy collection and analysis of data that can be readily processed to assess peer acceptance. Within this context, abundant research has been conducted on peer acceptance, and this has yielded the comprehensive development and refinement of theories of peer rejection. Likewise, with relatively recent advances in social network research, there has been an increase in studies that examine similarity in peer affiliations. From this work, researchers have been able to examine and extend theories of homophily, selective affiliation, and socialization (for example, Ennett & Bauman, 1994; Espelage, Green, & Wasserman, this volume; Kindermann, 1993). Although work in these areas is important and has been quite fruitful, other promising theories that are less methodologically accessible have not been as thoroughly examined or developed. Fortunately, the methods and procedures described in this volume are well suited for investigating several areas that are methodologically and theoretically complex but warrant more attention. Three examples are briefly described below.

One area of research that may benefit from the methodological and conceptual advances presented here is the expansion of the study of *social synchrony* in interpersonal interchanges and relationships. The concept of social synchrony refers to a property of social interactions in which "one person's acts are coordinated with and supportive of the ongoing activity of another individual" (Cairns, 1979 p. 298). *Reciprocity* is a form of synchrony that refers to similarity in actions by two or more individuals. This concept serves as a theoretical foundation for studies pertaining to homophily and socialization. Yet, a second form of social synchrony—*complementarity*—may be equally important for understanding group formation and process. Complementarity refers to actions in which the roles of two or more individuals are different but each is necessary for the ongoing activity of the other (for example, leader and follower). Although peer groups tend to be composed of individuals who are in some ways similar, they often contain members who are diverse on key characteristics and who may serve different but complementary social roles within the peer group (Farmer, Xie, Cairns, & Hutchins, 2007). For example, recent studies suggest that subtypes of aggressive youth such as popular aggressive and unpopular aggressive do not associate with each other but associate with peers who are similar to them in terms of perceived popularity (Farmer et al., 2002, 2003). Further, some aggressive youth appear to gain support from a range of conventional peers (see Rodkin, Farmer, Pearl, & Van Acker, 2006). These findings speak to both the strengths and the limitations of the homophily framework and may help explain why antisocial youth had rejected status in only two of eight schools (Light & Dishion, this volume).

However, complementarity is a difficult construct to assess and requires the analyses of interaction patterns and the assessment of social roles and hierarchies within peer groups. The Q-connectivity method (Hanish et al., this volume), the p* methodologies for conducting microlevel analyses of network structures (Espelage et al., this volume), and the analyses of network cohesiveness and status hierarchies (Gest et al., this volume) appear suitable for investigating key constructs associated with complementarity. By carefully bringing these methodologies together, it should be possible to generate new perspectives on how youth who are in some ways dissimilar come together to support each other and the broader peer group. In turn, such work should yield new conceptual views for examining continuity and fluidity in peer networks and classroom social structures.

A second area of research that can be enhanced by the work in these chapters involves variability in both classroom and school contexts. As a former special education teacher and current education professor, I have approached the study of social networks with the understanding that the mix of students in a classroom or school can strongly influence instructional engagement and classroom behavior. More recently, in conducting research in rural communities across the country, I have become aware of the tremendous variability in school configurations and contexts. However, much of the work on peer relations and social networks has assumed a "typical" classroom and school framework. As Rodkin et al. (this volume) demonstrate, peer groups processes systematically vary in relation to the composition of classrooms. Furthermore, as Light and Dishion (this volume) find, variability in social relations is evident at the school level. Together, these studies highlight the importance of developing measurement and analytic approaches that preserve information about the context. Although multilevel techniques can promote awareness of ecological influences, there is also a need to develop techniques that facilitate the retention of "yoked" information or, in Cairns' terminology, the pattern of correlated constraints, linking individuals, groups, and schools in our studies of social processes. In addition to demonstrating what can be learned by examining variability within and across social contexts, these studies underscore the utility of exploring contextual differences as "natural" experiments in the study of social processes.

A third underexplored but critical issue in the study of individuals within the peer context involves clarifying developmental and organizational contributions. Schools are often organized in ways that reflect commonly held views about youths' social capacities and needs. Accordingly, the social contexts in preschool, elementary, middle, and high school settings tend to be quite distinct and are often designed around adults' conceptions of what is developmentally appropriate for a specific age group. As a result, some of the perceived developmental differences in children's social relations and processes may reflect differences in the social environments that we create for them at particular ages.

Much of the research on social networks has been initiated at the late childhood or early adolescent period. At times there seems to be a collective assumption that peer groups and social networks are not developmentally relevant until the late elementary school years. On this count, Rubin, Bukowski, and Parker (1998) document that there is a general lack of research on peer groups and structures in the early and middle childhood periods. However, with recent methodological advances, it is possible to identify network structures and peer group processes in the preschool and early elementary periods (for example, Hanish et al., this volume). Although it is too early for definitive judgments, it appears that some phenomena that have been viewed as being developmentally determined may, in fact, be linked to organizational and process factors. For example, Pellegrini et al. (2007) have shown that the network reshuffling and jockeying for social position found during the transition from elementary to middle school were also largely evident in the transition from preschool to elementary school. As new methods for analyzing social networks are further refined for use with younger populations, it is possible that new information will emerge to suggest revisions in current conceptualizations of the role of peer groups and hierarchical social structures in early childhood social development.

In conclusion, although the study of social networks and peer contexts has traditionally lingered behind research on individuals and friendships (see Cairns, Xie, & Leung, 1998), the chapters in this volume mark a significant shift in the field. The change is not simply one of interest and attention but rather, as the studies in this volume demonstrate, striking advances in social network research in terms of depth, sophistication, and scope. Although I cannot speak for Dr. Bronfenbrenner, Dr. Cairns, and others who have guided the study of peer group context, I expect they would be pleased not only by the work in this volume but also by the growing emphasis on social networks within the peer relations community. These are exciting times for conducting social network research, and I look forward to the new directions that the future holds.

References

Bronfenbrenner, U. (1943). A constant frame of reference for sociometric research. *Sociometry, 6,* 363–397.

Cairns, R. B. (1979). *Social development: The origins and plasticity of interchanges.* New York: Freeman.

Cairns, R. B., Xie, H. L., & Leung, M-C., (1998). The popularity of friendship and the neglect of social networks: Toward a new balance. In W. M. Bukowski & A.H.N. Cillessen (Eds.), *Sociometry then and now: Building on six decades of measuring children's experiences with the peer group* (pp. 25–53). San Francisco: Jossey-Bass.

Ennett, S. T., & Bauman, K. E. (1994). The contribution of influence and selection to adolescent peer group homogeneity: The case of adolescent cigarette smoking. *Journal of Personality and Social Psychology, 67,* 653–666.

Farmer, T. W., Estell, D. B., Bishop, J. L., O'Neal, K. K., & Cairns, B. D. (2003). Rejected bullies or popular leaders? The social relations of aggressive subtypes of rural African-American early adolescents. *Developmental Psychology, 39,* 992–1004.

Farmer, T. W., Leung, M. C., Pearl, R., Rodkin, P. C., Cadwallader, T. W., & Van Acker, R. (2002). Deviant or diverse peer groups? The peer affiliations of aggressive elementary students. *Journal of Educational Psychology, 94,* 611–620.

Farmer, T. W., Xie, H. L., Cairns, B. D., & Hutchins, B. C. (2007). Social synchrony, peer networks, and aggression in school. In P. Hawley, T. D. Little, & P. C. Rodkin (Eds.), *Aggression and adaptation: The bright side to bad behavior.* Mahwah, NJ: Erlbaum.

Kindermann, T. A. (1993). Natural peer groups as contexts for individual development: The case of children's motivation in school. *Developmental Psychology, 29,* 970–977.

Pellegrini, A. D., Roseth, C. J., Mliner, S., Bohn, C. M., Van Ryzin, M., Vance, N., et al. (2007). Social dominance in preschool classrooms. *Journal of Comparative Psychology, 121,* 54–64.

Rodkin, P. C., Farmer, T. W., Pearl, R., & Van Acker, R. (2006). They're cool: Social status and group support for aggressive boys and girls. *Social Development, 15,* 175–204.

Rubin, K. H., Bukowski, W. J., & Parker, J. G. (1998). Peer interactions, relationships, and groups. In W. Damon & N. Eisenberg (Eds.), *Handbook of child psychology* (5th ed., Vol. 3, pp. 619–700). Hoboken, NJ: Wiley.

THOMAS W. FARMER is associate professor of educational and school psychology and special education at the Pennsylvania State University.

Index

Aboud, F. E., 26, 28
Adler, P. A., 46, 56
Adler, P., 46, 56
African American and European American children, 4–5, 25–40, 103
Ageton, S. S., 78
Ahn, H.-J., 4, 25, 42, 94
Amazeen, P. G., 79
Anders, M. C., 18
Antisocial behavior and peer rejection, 77–87
Apostoleris, N. H., 45
Asher, S. R., 27, 28, 47
Axelrod, J. L., 72

Back, K., 87
Bailey, C. A., 61
Bandura, A., 17
Barbaranelli, C., 17
Barcelo, H., 9, 10, 11, 23
Barth, J. M., 27
Bauman, K. E., 65, 79, 86, 105
Bellmore, A. D., 26
Benenson, J. F., 45, 56
Berthelsen, D., 97
Bierman, K. L., 96
Birch, S. H., 4, 17
Bishop, J. L., 104
Bjorklund, D. F., 72
Björkqvist, K., 62
Blake, J. J., 27, 28, 39
Board of Education of Topeka, Brown v., 26, 40
Boivin, M., 21, 96
Bonacich, P., 50
Borch, C., 98
Borgatti, S. P., 44
Boulton, M. J., 72
Boys' and girls' peer networks, 5, 43–57
Brendgen, M., 61
Bronfenbrenner, U., 2, 6, 71, 101–102, 107
Brooks, D., 25, 26, 39
Brown v. Board of Education of Topeka, 26
Brown, B. B., 27, 92
Brushi, C., 96
Buhs, E. S., 4, 17

Bukowski, W. M., 2, 62, 72, 91, 92
Bullock, B. M., 86
Bully Scale, Illinois, 64
Bullying behavior, 3, 62–63, 65, 67, 69–70, 72
Burraston, B., 86
Butner, J., 79
Butts, C. T., 49

Cadwallader, T. W., 104
Cairns, B. D., 10, 47, 48, 62, 77, 92, 104, 105
Cairns, R. B., 2, 4, 6, 10, 18, 28, 47, 48, 62, 77, 92, 107
Caldwell, K. A., 72
Campbell, M. E., 27
Caprara, G. V., 17, 21
Card, N. A., 40, 92
Catherwood, D., 97
Chambers, S. M., 21
Chang, L., 26, 62
Charlesworth, W. R., 46, 56
Cheatham, C. L., 56
Cillessen, A.H.N., 2, 6, 91, 92, 97, 98, 100
Clark, K. B., 26
Clark, M. P., 26
Coie, J. D., 78, 92, 96
Coleman, J. S., 4, 6, 45
Complementarity, 105
Connolly, J. A., 61
Cook, J. M., 62
Cook, W. L., 93
Coolahan, K. C., 18
Criswell, J. H., 26

Davidson, A. J., 43, 48, 59, 94
De Kemp, R., 86
Degirmencioglu, S. M., 92
Demaray, M. K., 72
Den Exter Blokland, E., 86
Deschenes, E. P., 61
Dishion, T. J., 3, 6, 61, 77, 78, 81, 86, 89, 92, 94, 95, 96, 103, 105
Distinctiveness of groups, 44, 47, 49–50, 52
Dodge, K. A., 3, 61, 77, 78, 96
Dubois, D. L., 27

109

Dunn, L. M., 19
Dunn, L. M., 19
Dunphy, D. C., 45
Dzur, C., 46, 56

Edelman, M. S., 45
Eder, D., 46, 57, 62
Elliott, D., 78
Engels, R.C.M., 86
Ennett, S. T., 65, 79, 86, 105
Esbensen, F. A., 61
Espelage, D. L., 3, 5, 6, 18, 61, 62, 64, 65, 72, 75, 92, 94, 95, 96, 103, 105
Estell, D. B., 104

Fabes, R. A., 3, 4, 9, 11, 12, 18, 21, 24, 43, 45, 56
Fagot, B. I., 18
Fantuzzo, J. W., 18
Farmer, T., 6, 28, 33, 39, 48, 78, 85, 101, 104, 105, 108
Farver, J.A.M., 62
Faust, K., 44, 50, 80
Festinger, L., 87
Fisher, L. A., 79
Frankowski, R., 64
Freeman, L. C., 2, 44, 49

Gariepy, J. L., 10, 47, 62, 92
Gatlin, D., 27
Gearhart, M., 21
Gest, S. D., 5, 10, 28, 43, 47, 48, 59, 62, 92, 94, 95, 96, 97, 98, 103
Giammarino, M., 96
Gifford-Smith, M., 61, 77
Girls' and boys' peer networks, 5, 43–57
Gold, M., 78
Goodreau, S. M., 49
Goodwin, M. H., 46, 56
Gorard, S., 30
Graham, S., 25, 26, 27, 97, 98
Graham-Bermann, S. A., 28
Granic, I., 95
Green, H., 5, 6, 61, 62, 63, 75, 105
Green, V. A., 94, 97
Greenberg, D. F., 78
Griesler, P. C., 61, 77
Guay, F., 21
Guberman, S. R., 21
Gunnar, M. R., 56

Hallinan, M. T., 26, 27, 28, 46, 49, 57
Hamm, J. V., 27
Handcock, M. S., 49

Hanish, L. D., 1, 3, 4, 8, 9, 11, 12, 13, 18, 21, 23, 26, 43, 94, 95, 96, 102, 105, 107
Hannan, K. J., 79
Hartup, W. W., 28, 78
Hausman, L. R., 25
Hawley, P. H., 40, 72
Haynie, D. L., 62, 71
Heck, D. J., 27
Henkel, R., 3, 18, 62, 92
Herald, S. L., 17
Herzog, M., 3
Hinde, R. A., 11
Hirsch, B. J., 27
Hodges, E.V.E., 21, 40, 72, 92
Hollowell, J. H., 78
Holmwall, J., 9, 24
Holt, M., 3, 18, 62, 64, 92
Homophily, 5–6, 62–63, 67, 72
Huisman, M., 78, 96
Huizinga, D., 78
Hunter, D. R., 49
Hutchins, B. C., 105
Huttunen, A., 3

Inder, P. M., 46, 56
Individuals, dyads, and groups, 91–92, 98
Irving, K., 97

Jacklin, C. N., 44, 57
Jackson, M. F., 27, 28, 39
Jennings, H., 2, 6
Johnson, R. J., 61
Judd, C. M., 79
Juvonen, J., 26, 27

Kalish, Y., 5
Kaplan, H. B., 61
Kashy, D. A., 93
Kaukiainen, A., 62
Kavanagh, K., 78
Keefe, P. R., 1
Kenny, D. A., 79, 93
Kessler, R. C., 78
Kindermann, T. A., 3, 9, 92, 105
Kistner, J., 27, 28
Kless, S., 46
Kochel, K. P., 17
Kumpulainen, K., 21
Kupersmidt, J. B., 78

Labenbacher, R., 10, 11
Ladd, G. W., 4, 17, 18, 21, 26

LaFontana, K. M., 97
Lagerspetz, K.M.J., 3, 62
Lansford, J. E., 3
Leaper, C., 43, 44, 57
Lease, A. M., 27, 28, 39
Lease, M. L., 72
Leonard, S., 3
Leung, M-C., 2, 28, 104, 107
Light, J., 6, 77, 81, 89, 94, 95, 96, 103, 105
Little, T. D., 40
Lochman, J. E., 27
Loeber, R., 61
Lohr, M. J., 92
Long, J., 72
Lusher, D., 5

Maccoby, E. E., 3, 5, 21, 43, 44, 55, 56, 57
Madden-Derdich, D. A., 18
Malecki, C. K., 72
Manz, P. H., 18
Marsden, P. V., 79
Martin, C. L., 3, 4, 9, 11, 12, 18, 21, 23, 43
Mather, K., 18
McCord, J., 61, 92
McGrew, K. S., 18
McNelles, L. R., 61
McPerson, M., 62
Mendelson, M. J., 26
Merten, D. E., 46, 56
Metzler, A., 27
Miller, P. H., 95
Moody, J., 27, 28, 30, 43, 48, 49, 60, 94
Moreno, J. L., 2, 6, 26
Morris, M., 49
Moss, A., 21
Mulvey, G. M., 79
Muñoz-Sandoval, A. F., 18
Murray, D. M., 79
Musgrove, K. T., 72
Mutanen, M., 21

Neckerman, H. J., 10, 47, 62, 77, 92
Nelson, S. E., 78, 86
Nenga, S. K., 62
Nesdale, D., 62, 72
Newcomb, A. F., 62
Nishina, A., 27

Ojala, K., 62, 72
Olson, S. L., 77
Omark, D. R., 45

O'Neal, K. K., 104
Orpinas, P., 64
Osterman, K., 62

p^* analysis, 5, 61, 63, 65, 66, 67, 70, 71, 94, 103
Palermo, F., 9, 24
Parad, H. W., 96
Parents Involved in Community Schools v. Seattle School District, No. 1, 25
Parker, J. G., 28, 45, 47, 49, 91
Parnass, J., 45
Pastorelli, C., 17
Patterson, G. R., 61, 77, 95
Pattison, P., 5, 65
Pearce, S. L., 56
Pearl, R., 28, 33, 39, 78, 85, 104, 105
Peer networks, girls' and boys', 43–57
Peer rejection and antisocial behavior, 77–87
Peer relations, new trends in study of, 94–95
Pellegrini, A. D., 62, 72, 107
Perrin, J. E., 48
Perry, D. G., 72
Pilgrim, C., 92
Poteat, P., 62, 63, 65
Poulin, F., 86, 92
Powell, N., 27
Preschoolers' involvement with groups of peers, 9–22
Prinstein, M. J., 79
Purdy, K. T., 26

Q-connectivity method, 4, 10, 11–22, 94, 96, 102, 105
Quillian, L., 26, 27

Renshaw, P. D., 2
Rice, R. E., 10
Richards, W. D., 10
Risi, S., 27
Robins, G., 5, 63, 65
Rodkin, P. C., 1, 3, 4, 8, 25, 28, 33, 39, 40, 42, 78, 85, 94, 95, 97, 98, 103, 104, 105
Rose, A. J., 43, 44, 49, 55
Rubin, K. H., 91
Rudolph, K. D., 43, 44, 49, 55
Rulison, K. L., 43, 48, 60, 94
Ryan, A., 3, 4

Salmivalli, C., 3, 62
Savin-Williams, R. C., 45

Saxe, G. B., 21
Schachter, S., 87
Schofield, J. W., 25
Scholt, R.H.J., 86
Schwartz, D., 62
Schweinberger, M., 78, 79, 96
Scott, J., 44
Seal, J., 45, 49
Seattle School District, No. 1, Parents Involved in Community Schools v., 25
Sebanc, A. M., 56
Seidman, E., 26
Self-selection, 62, 63
Sherif, M., 2, 3, 6
SIENA modeling, 6, 79, 80, 83, 84, 85, 94, 95, 103
Singleton, L. C., 27, 28
Sippola, L. K., 62
Smith, A. B., 46, 56
Smith, L. B., 95
Smith, T., 57
Smith-Lovin, L., 62
Snijders, T.A.B., 78, 79, 81, 95
Social cognitive map (SCM) method, 48, 50, 103
Social development and social network analysis, 1–7
Social networks: challenges in study of, 92–93; new perspectives on, 95–98; as opportunity for integration, 93–94
Social synchrony, 105
Steglich, C.E.G., 78, 79, 95
Stevenson-Hinde, J., 11
Stormshak, E. A., 81, 83, 85, 96
Stouthamer-Loeber, M., 61
Sutton-Smith, B., 18

Tajfel, H., 26, 62
Taylor, C., 30

Thelen, E., 95
Thorne, B., 46, 56
Tight-knittedness of networks, 44, 47, 49, 50–52, 53, 54, 57
Tremblay, R. E., 61
Tseng, V., 26
Turner, J. C., 62
Two-cultures theory, 5, 44, 55, 57

Underwood, M., 43, 44, 45, 47, 57
Urberg, K. A., 92

Van Acker, R., 28, 33, 39, 78, 85, 104, 105
Vitaro, F., 61, 86
Voeten, M., 62

Walker, D. L., 28
Wang, P., 65
Wang, S. S., 79
Wasserman, S., 5, 6, 44, 50, 61, 63, 75, 80, 94, 105
Welsh, J. A., 43, 48, 60, 94
Wentzel, K. R., 72
Williams, J., 25
Wilson, T., 3, 4, 25, 42, 94
Winter, C., 86
Witkow, M. R., 26
Woodcock, R. W., 18
Wright, J. C., 96

Xie, H., 2, 28, 48, 105, 107
Xu, Y., 62

Yasui, M., 81
Yoerger, K., 61

Zimbardo, P. G., 17

OTHER TITLES AVAILABLE IN THE
NEW DIRECTIONS FOR CHILD AND ADOLESCENT DEVELOPMENT SERIES
*Reed W. Larson and Lene Arnett Jensen, Editors-in-Chief
William Damon, Founding Editor-in-Chief*

For a complete list of back issues, please visit www.josseybass..com/go/ndcad

CAD 117 **Attachment in Adolescence: Reflections and New Angles**
Miri Scharf, Ofra Mayseless, Editors
In recent years, the number of empirical studies examining attachment in adolescence has grown considerably, with most focusing on individual differences in attachment security. This volume goes a step further in extending our knowledge and understanding. The physical, cognitive, emotional, and social changes that characterize adolescence invite a closer conceptual look at attachment processes and organization during this period. The chapter authors, leading researchers in attachment in adolescence, address key topics in attachment processes in adolescence. These include issues such as the normative distancing from parents and the growing importance of peers, the formation of varied attachment hierarchies, the changing nature of attachment dynamics from issues of survival to issues of affect regulation, siblings' similarity in attachment representations, individual differences in social information processes in adolescence, and stability and change in attachment representations in a risk sample. Together the chapters provide a compelling discussion of intriguing issues and broaden our understanding of attachment in adolescence and the basic tenets of attachment theory at large.
ISBN: 978-04702-25608

CAD 116 **Linking Parents and Family to Adolescent Peer Relations: Ethnic and Cultural Considerations**
B. Bradford Brown, Nina S. Mounts, Editors
Ethnic and cultural background shapes young people's development and behavior in a variety of ways, including their interactions with family and peers. The intersection of family and peer worlds during childhood has been studied extensively, but only recently has this work been extended to adolescence. This volume of *New Directions for Child and Adolescent Development* highlights new research linking family to adolescent peer relations from a multiethnic perspective. Using qualitative and quantitative research methods, the contributors consider similarities and differences within and between ethnic groups in regard to several issues: parents' goals and strategies for guiding young people to adaptive peer relationships, how peer relationships shape and are shaped by kin relationships, and the specific strategies that adolescents and parents use to manage information about peers or negotiate rules about peer interactions and relationships. Findings emphasize the central role played by sociocultural context in shaping the complex, bidirectional processes that link family members to adolescents' peer social experiences.
ISBN 978-04701-78010

CAD 115 **Conventionality in Cognitive Development: How Children Acquire Shared Representations in Language, Thought, and Action**
Chuck W. Kalish, Mark A. Sabbagh, Editors
An important part of cognitive development is coming to think in culturally normative ways. Children learn the right names for objects, proper functions for tools, appropriate ways to categorize, and the rules for games. In each of

these cases, what makes a given practice normative is not naturally given. There is not necessarily any objectively better or worse way to do any of these things. Instead, what makes them correct is that people agree on how they should be done, and each of these practices therefore has an important conventional basis. The chapters in this volume highlight the fact that successful participation in practices of language, cognition, and play depends on children's ability to acquire representations that other members of their social worlds share. Each of these domains poses problems of identifying normative standards and achieving coordination across agents. This volume brings together scholars from diverse areas in cognitive development to consider the psychological mechanisms supporting the use and acquisition of conventional knowledge.
ISBN 978-07879-96970

CAD 114 **Respect and Disrespect: Cultural and Developmental Origins**
David W. Schwalb, Barbara J. Schwalb, Editors
Respect enables children and teenagers to value other people, institutions, traditions, and themselves. Disrespect is the agent that dissolves positive relationships and fosters hostile and cynical relationships. Unfortunately, parents, educators, children, and adolescents in many societies note with alarm a growing problem of disrespect and a decline in respect for self and others. Is this disturbing trend a worldwide problem? To answer this question, we must begin to study the developmental and cultural origins of respect and disrespect. Five research teams report that respect and disrespect are influenced by experiences in the family, school, community, and, most importantly, the broader cultural setting. The chapters introduce a new topic area for mainstream developmental sciences that is relevant to the interests of scholars, educators, practitioners, and policymakers.
ISBN 978-07879-95584

CAD 113 **The Modernization of Youth Transitions in Europe**
Manuela du Bois-Reymond, Lynne Chisholm, Editors
This compelling volume focuses on what it is like to be young in the rapidly changing, enormously diverse world region that is early 21st century Europe. Designed for a North American readership interested in youth and young adulthood, *The Modernization of Youth Transitions in Europe* provides a rich fund of theoretical insight and empirical evidence about the implications of contemporary modernization processes for young people living, learning, and working across Europe. Chapters have been specially written for this volume by well-known youth sociologists; they cover a wide range of themes against a shared background of the reshaping of the life course and its constituent phases toward greater openness and contigency. New modes of learning accompany complex routes into employment and career under rapidly changing labor market conditions and occupational profiles, while at the same time new family and lifestyle forms are developing alongside greater intergenerational responsibilities in the face of the retreat of the modern welfare state. The complex patterns of change for today's young Europeans are set into a broader framework that analyzes the emergence and character of European youth research and youth policy in recent years.
ISBN 978-07879-88890

CAD 112 **Rethinking Positive Adolescent Female Sexual Development**
Lisa M. Diamond, Editor
This volume provides thoughtful and diverse perspectives on female adolescent sexuality. These perspectives integrate biological, cultural, and interpersonal influences on adolescent girls' sexuality, and highlight the importance of using multiple methods to investigate sexual ideation and experience. Tra-

ditional portrayals cast adolescent females as sexual gatekeepers whose primary task is to fend off boys' sexual overtures and set aside their own sexual desires in order to reduce their risks for pregnancy and sexually transmitted diseases. Yet an increasing number of thoughtful and constructive critiques have challenged this perspective, arguing for more sensitive, in-depth, multimethod investigations into the positive meanings of sexuality for adolescent girls that will allow us to conceptualize (and, ideally, advocate for) healthy sexual-developmental trajectories. Collectively, authors of this volume take up this movement and chart exciting new directions for the next generation of developmental research on adolescent female sexuality.
ISBN 978-07879-87350

CAD111 **Family Mealtime as a Context for Development and Socialization**
Reed W. Larson, Angela R. Wiley, Kathryn R. Branscomb, Editors
This issue examines the impact of family mealtime on the psychological development of young people. In the popular media, family mealtime is often presented as a vital institution for the socialization and development of young people, but also as one that is "going the way of the dinosaur." Although elements such as fast food and TV have become a part of many family mealtimes, evidence is beginning to suggest that mealtimes can also provide rich opportunities for children's and adolescents' development. While what happens at mealtimes varies greatly among families, an outline of the forms and functions of mealtimes is beginning to emerge from this research. In this issue, leading mealtime researchers from the fields of history, cultural anthropology, psycholinguistics, psychology, and nutrition critically review findings from each of their disciplines, giving primary focus on family mealtimes in the United States. The authors in this issue examine the history of family mealtimes, describe contemporary mealtime practices, elucidate the differing transactional processes that occur, and evaluate evidence on the outcomes associated with family mealtimes from children and adolescents.
ISBN 978-07879-85776

CAD 110 **Leaks in the Pipeline to Math, Science, and Technology Careers**
Janis E. Jacobs, Sandra D. Simpkins, Editors
Around the world, the need for highly trained scientists and technicians remains high, especially for positions that require employees to have a college degree and skills in math, science, and technology. The pipeline into these jobs begins in high school, but many "leaks" occur before young people reach the highly educated workforce needed to sustain leadership in science and technology. Students drop out of the educational pipeline in science and technology at alarming rates at each educational transition beginning in high school, but women and ethnic minority youth drop out at a faster rate. Women and minorities are consistently underrepresented in science and engineering courses and majors. They account for a small portion of the work force in high-paying and more innovative jobs that require advanced degrees. This schism between the skills necessary in our ever changing economy and the skill set that most young adults acquire is troubling. It leads us to ask the question that forms the basis for this issue: Why are adolescents and young adults, particularly women and minorities, opting out of the math, science, and technology pipeline? The volume addresses gender and ethnic differences in the math, science, and technology pipeline from multiple approaches, including theoretical perspectives, a review of the work in this field, presentation of findings from four longitudinal studies, and a discussion of research implications given the current educational and economic climate.
ISBN 978-07879-83932

CAD 109 **New Horizons in Developmental Theory and Research**
Lene Arnett Jensen, Reed W. Larson, Editors
This inaugural issue by the new editors-in-chief brings together a group of cutting-edge developmental scholars who each report on promising new lines of theory and research within their specialty areas. Their essays cover a selection of important topics including emotion-regulation, family socialization, friendship, self, civic engagement, media, and culture. In the succinct, engaging essays, all authors provide thought-provoking views of the horizons in the field.
ISBN 978-07879-83413

CAD 108 **Changing Boundaries of Parental Authority During Adolescence**
Judith Smetena, Editor
This volume describes research focusing on changes in different dimensions of parenting and conceptions of parental authority during adolescence. The seven chapters illuminate the dimensions of parenting that change (or remain stable) over the course of adolescence. The chapters also ighlight the importance of considering variations in parenting accoding to the different domains of adolescents' lives, their relationships to the development of responsibility automony, and how these are influenced by socioeconomic status, culture, and ethnicity. Thus, the chapters in this volume provide new directions for conceptualizing variations in parenting over the second decade of life and their implicaions for adolescent adjustment and well-being. The authors point to the need for developmentally sensitive models of parenting that consider changes within domains over time, their influence on adolescent development and functioning, and potential asynchronies between parents and adolescents.
ISBN 978-07879-81921

CAD 107 **The Experience of Close Friendship in Adolescence**
Niobe Way, Jill V. Hamm, Editors
In this issue, we present findings from four studies that employed qualitative methodology to gain insight into the how and the why of close friendships. How do adolescents experience trust and intimacy in their friendships? Why are these relational experiences critical for emotional adjustment? And how does the social and cultural context shape the ways in which adolescents experience their close friendships? The studies reveal the ways in which adolescents from diverse cultural backgrounds speak about their close friendships and the individual and contextual factors that shape and are shaped by their experiences of close friendships.
ISBN 978-07879-80573

CAD 106 **Social and Self Process Underlying Math and Science Achievement**
Heather Bouchey, Cynthia Winston, Editors
In general, America's students are not faring well in science and mathematics. The chapters in this volume employ novel conceptual and empirical approaches to investigate how social and individual factors interact to effect successful math and science achievement. Each of the chapters is solidly grounded in theory and provides new insight concerning the integration of student-level and contextual influences. Inclusion of youth from diverse socioeconomic and ethnic backgrounds is a salient feature of the volume.
ISBN 978-07879-79164

CAD 105 **Human Technogenesis: Cultural Pathways Through the Information Age**
Dinesh Sharma, Editor
The technologically driven information economy is reshaping everyday human behavior and sociocultural environments. Yet our paradigms for

understanding human development within a cultural framework are guided by traditional and dichotomous ideas about the social world (for example, individualism-collectivism, egocentric-sociocentric, modern-traditional, Western-Non-Western). As the impact of information technologies permeates all aspects of our lives, research in human development and psychology must face the digitally, connected social environments as its laboratory, filled with naturally occurring experiments, whether it is the speed at which we now communicate in the home or workplace, the far-reaching access children have to a wide array of information previously unavailable, or the vicarious anonymity with which we are able to participate in each other's lives through the new media tools. The chapters in this volume claim that the recent wave of innovation and adaptation to information technologies, giving rise to a new form of "human technogenesis," is fundamentally transforming our everyday interactions and potentially reconstructing the nature and process of human development. Human technogenesis is the constructive process of individual and sociocultural innovation and adaptation to the everyday interactions with information technologies, which significantly affects the developing and the developed mind.
ISBN 978-07879-77795

CAD 104 **Culture and Developing Selves: Beyond Dichotomization**
Michael F. Mascolo, Jin Li, Editors
The distinction between individualism and collectivism (I-C) has been useful in understanding differences in the world's cultures and the developing selves that they spawn. From this view, within Individualist (most North American and Western-European) cultures, individuals develop a sense of self as separate, autonomous, and independent of others. In contrast, collectivist cultures (for example, many Asian cultures) place primary value on group orientation, the goals and needs of others, and readiness to cooperate. However, despite its utility, the I-C dimension can obscure an analysis of the complexity of selves that develop in individualist and collectivist cultures. Individuality and interiority are represented in selves that develop within cultures considered collectivistic; conversely; selves in individualist cultures are defined through relations with others. The contributors to this volume examine the multiplicity of developing selfhood that exists within and between cultures. In so doing, the contributors examine the coexistence of self-cultivation and social obligation among the Chinese, the coexistence of deep spiritual interiority and social duty in urban India, changing patterns of identity in immigrant families, and how autonomy functions in the service of social relations among American adolescents. It is argued that individuality and connectedness cannot exist independent of each other. Although there are dramatic differences in how they are constructed, individual and communal dimensions of selfhood must be represented in some form in selves that develop in all cultures.
ISBN 978-07879-76262

CAD 103 **Connections Between Theory of Mind and Sociomoral Development**
Jodie A. Baird, Bryan W. Sokol
The heightened attention to research on theory of mind is due in large part to the shared intuition that this core aspect of development must have important consequences for, and connections with, children's evolving social competence. This seems particularly true for the moral domain, where a psychological, or inward, focus is often taken to be a constitutive feature of what distinguishes moral actions from other kinds of behavior. Unfortunately, the theory-of-mind enterprise has largely failed to capitalize on this fundamental connection between mental life and morality, and, as a result, it has been

effectively cut off from the study of sociomoral development. The chapters in this volume represent different, though complementary, attempts to bridge the gap that exists between these research traditions. Two central questions are addressed. First, what is the impact of children's conceptions of the mind on their moral judgements? Second, does children's mental state understanding influence the moral quality of their own behavior? In the concluding chapters, prominent scholars from both the theory-of-mind literature and the moral development domain comment on the efforts being made to link these research traditions and offer suggestions for future inquiry.
ISBN 978-07879-74404

CAD 102 *Enemies and the Darker Side of Peer Relations*
Ernest V. Hodges, Noel A. Card, Editors
The darker side of peer relations is subject that has been largely ignored by researchers. This volume begins the much-needed theoretical and empirically based explorations of the factors involved in the foremation, maintenance, and impact of enemies and other mutual antipathies. Using diverse samples, the chapter authors provide an empirically based exposition of factors relevant to the formation and maintenance of these relations, as well as their developmental impact. Both distal (for example, attachment styles with parents, community violence exposure) and proximal (for example, perceptions of enemies' behavior, social structure of the peer group) factors related to inimical relations are explored, and the developmental sequelaw (for example, affective, behavioral, interpersonal) of having enemies are examined with concurrent and longitudinal designs.
ISBN 978-07879-72721

CAD 101 *Person-Centered Approaches to Studying Development in Context*
Stephen C. Peck, Robert W. Roeser, Editors
This volume introduces readers to theoretical and methodological discussions, along with empirical illustrations, of using pattern-centered analyses in studying development in context. Pattern-centered analytic techniques refer to a family of research tools that identify patterns or profiles of variables within individuals and thereby classify individuals into homogeneous subgroups based on their similarity of profile. These techniques find their theoretical foundation in holistic, developmental systems theories in which notions of organization, process dynamics, interactions and transactions, context, and life course development are focal. The term *person-centered* is used to contrast with the traditional emphasis on variables; the term *pattern-centered* is used to extend the principles of person-centered approaches to other levels of analysis (for example, social context). Contributors present the theoretical foundations of pattern-centered analytic techniques, describe specific tools that may be of use to developmentalists interested in using such techniques and provide four empirical illustrations of their use in relation to educational achievement and attainments, aggressive behavior and social popularity, and alcohol use during the childhood and adolescent periods.
ISBN 978-07879-71694

CAD 100 *Exploring Cultural Conceptions of the Transitions to Adulthood*
Jeffrey Jensen Arnett, Editor
The transition to adulthood has been studied for decades in terms of transition events such as leaving home, finishing education, and entering marriage and parenthood, but only recently have studies examined the conceptions of young people themselves on what it means to become an adult. The goal

of this volume is to extend the study of conceptions of adulthood to a wider range of cultures. The chapters in this volume examine conceptions of adulthood among Israelis, Argentines, American Mormons, Germans, Canadians, and three American ethnic minority groups. There is a widespread emphasis across cultures on individualistic criteria for adulthood, but each culture has been found to emphasize culturally distinctive criteria as well. This volume represents a beginning in research on cultural conceptions of the transition to adulthood and points the way to a broad range of opportunities for future investigation.
ISBN 978-07879-69813

CAD 99 **Examining Adolescent Leisure Time Across Cultures: Developmental Opportunities and Risks**
Suman Verma, Reed W. Larson, Editors
Adolescence worldwide is a life period of role restructuring and social learning. Free-time activities provide opportunities to experiment with roles and develop new adaptive strategies and other interpersonal skills that have an impact on development, socialization, and the transition to adulthood. Leisure provides a rich context in which adolescents can gain control over their attentional processes and learn from relationships with peers, but it also has potential costs, such as involvement in deviant and risk behaviors. To gain deeper insight into the developmental opportunities and risks that adolescents experience in their free time, this volume explores adolescents' daily leisure experience across countries. Each chapter describes the sociocultural contexts in which adolescents live, along with a profile of free-time activities. Collectively, the chapters highlight the differences and similarities between cultures; how family, peers, and wider social factors influence the use of free time; which societies provide more freedom and at what costs; and how adolescents cope with restricted degrees of freedom and with what consequences on their mental health and well-being.
ISBN 978-07879-68366

New Directions for Child & Adolescent Development
Order Form
SUBSCRIPTIONS AND SINGLE ISSUES

DISCOUNTED BACK ISSUES:

*Use this form to receive **20% off** all back issues of New Directions for Child & Adolescent Development. All single issues priced at **$23.20** (normally $29.00)*

TITLE	ISSUE NO.	ISBN
_____	_____	_____
_____	_____	_____

Call 888-378-2537 or see mailing instructions below. When calling, mention the promotional code, **JB7ND**, to receive your discount.
For a complete list of issues, please visit www.josseybass.com/go/ndcad

SUBSCRIPTIONS: (1 year, 4 issues)

☐ New Order   ☐ Renewal

U.S.	☐ Individual: $85	☐ Institutional: $258
Canada/Mexico	☐ Individual: $85	☐ Institutional: $298
All Others	☐ Individual: $109	☐ Institutional: $332

Call 888-378-2537 or see mailing and pricing instructions below. Online subscriptions are available at www.interscience.wiley.com.

Copy or detach page and send to:
John Wiley & Sons, Journals Dept, 5th Floor
989 Market Street, San Francisco, CA 94103-1741

Order Form can also be faxed to: 888-481-2665

Issue/Subscription Amount: $ _____	**SHIPPING CHARGES:**		
Shipping Amount: $ _____	SURFACE	Domestic	Canadian
(for single issues only—subscription prices include shipping)	First Item	$5.00	$6.00
Total Amount: $ _____	Each Add'l Item	$3.00	$1.50

(No sales tax for U.S. subscriptions. Canadian residents, add GST for subscription orders. Individual rate subscriptions must be paid by personal check or credit card. Individual rate subscriptions may not be resold as library copies.)

☐ Payment enclosed (U.S. check or money order only. All payments must be in U.S. dollars.)
☐ VISA ☐ MC ☐ Amex # _____ Exp. Date _____
Card Holder Name _____ Card Issue # _____
Signature _____ Day Phone _____
☐ Bill Me (U.S. institutional orders only. Purchase order required.)
Purchase order # _____
         Federal Tax ID13559302   GST 89102 8052

Name _____
Address _____
Phone _____ E-mail _____

JB7ND

NEW DIRECTIONS FOR CHILD AND ADOLESCENT DEVELOPMENT IS NOW AVAILABLE ONLINE AT WILEY INTERSCIENCE

What is Wiley InterScience?

Wiley InterScience is the dynamic online content service from John Wiley & Sons delivering the full text of over 300 leading scientific, technical, medical, and professional journals, plus major reference works, the acclaimed Current Protocols laboratory manuals, and even the full text of select Wiley print books online.

What are some special features of Wiley InterScience?

Wiley Interscience Alerts is a service that delivers table of contents via e-mail for any journal available on Wiley InterScience as soon as a new issue is published online.
EarlyView is Wiley's exclusive service presenting individual articles online as soon as they are ready, even before the release of the compiled print issue. These articles are complete, peer-reviewed, and citable.
CrossRef is the innovative multi-publisher reference linking system enabling readers to move seamlessly from a reference in a journal article to the cited publication, typically located on a different server and published by a different publisher.

How can I access Wiley InterScience?

Visit http://www.interscience.wiley.com.

Guest Users can browse Wiley InterScience for unrestricted access to journal tables of contents and article abstracts, or use the powerful search engine.
Registered Users are provided with a *Personal Home Page* to store and manage customized alerts, searches, and links to favorite journals and articles. Additionally, Registered Users can view free online sample issues and preview selected material from major reference works.
Licensed Customers are entitled to access full-text journal articles in PDF, with select journals also offering full-text HTML.

How do I become an Authorized User?

Authorized Users are individuals authorized by a paying Customer to have access to the journals in Wiley InterScience. For example, a university that subscribes to Wiley journals is considered to be the Customer.
Faculty, staff, and students authorized by the university to have access to those journals in Wiley InterScience are Authorized Users. Users should contact their library for information on which Wiley journals they have access to in Wiley InterScience.

ASK YOUR INSTITUTION ABOUT WILEY INTERSCIENCE TODAY!

UNITED STATES POSTAL SERVICE — **Statement of Ownership, Management, and Circulation**
(All Periodicals Publications Except Requester Publications)

1. Publication Title	2. Publication Number	3. Filing Date
New Directions for Child and Adolescent Development	1 5 2 0 - 3 2 4 7	10/1/2007

4. Issue Frequency	5. Number of Issues Published Annually	6. Annual Subscription Price
Quarterly	4	$258

7. Complete Mailing Address of Known Office of Publication (Not printer) (Street, city, county, state, and ZIP+4®)

Wiley Subscriptions Services, Inc. at Jossey-Bass, 989 Market St., San Francisco, CA 94103

Contact Person: Joe Schuman
Telephone (Include area code): 415-782-3232

8. Complete Mailing Address of Headquarters or General Business Office of Publisher (Not printer)

Wiley Subscriptions Services, Inc., 111 River Street, Hoboken, NJ 07030

9. Full Names and Complete Mailing Addresses of Publisher, Editor, and Managing Editor (Do not leave blank)

Publisher (Name and complete mailing address)

Wiley Subscriptions Services, Inc., A Wiley Company at San Francisco, 989 Market St., San Francisco, CA 94103-1741

Editor (Name and complete mailing address)

Co-Editor - Reed Larson, Dept. of Human & Community Devel., Univ. of Illinois, 1105 W. Nevada St., Urbana IL 61801

Managing Editor (Name and complete mailing address)

Co-Editor - Dr. Lene Arnett Jensen, Ph.D., Clark University, Dept. of Psychology, 950 Main St., Worcester, MA 01610

10. Owner (Do not leave blank. If the publication is owned by a corporation, give the name and address of the corporation immediately followed by the names and addresses of all stockholders owning or holding 1 percent or more of the total amount of stock. If not owned by a corporation, give the names and addresses of the individual owners. If owned by a partnership or other unincorporated firm, give its name and address as well as those of each individual owner. If the publication is published by a nonprofit organization, give its name and address.)

Full Name	Complete Mailing Address
Wiley Subscriptions Services	111 River Street, Hoboken, NJ
(see attached list)	

11. Known Bondholders, Mortgagees, and Other Security Holders Owning or Holding 1 Percent or More of Total Amount of Bonds, Mortgages, or Other Securities. If none, check box ☒ None

Full Name	Complete Mailing Address

12. Tax Status (For completion by nonprofit organizations authorized to mail at nonprofit rates) (Check one)
The purpose, function, and nonprofit status of this organization and the exempt status for federal income tax purposes
☐ Has Not Changed During Preceding 12 Months
☐ Has Changed During Preceding 12 Months (Publisher must submit explanation of change with this statement)

13. Publication Title	14. Issue Date for Circulation Data
New Directions for Child and Adolescent Development	Summer 2007

15. Extent and Nature of Circulation		Average No. Copies Each Issue During Preceding 12 Months	No. Copies of Single Issue Published Nearest to Filing Date
a. Total Number of Copies (Net press run)		823	799
b. Paid Circulation (By Mail and Outside the Mail)	(1) Mailed Outside-County Paid Subscriptions Stated on PS Form 3541 (Include paid distribution above nominal rate, advertiser's proof copies, and exchange copies)	222	215
	(2) Mailed In-County Paid Subscriptions Stated on PS Form 3541 (Include paid distribution above nominal rate, advertiser's proof copies, and exchange copies)	0	0
	(3) Paid Distribution Outside the Mails Including Sales Through Dealers and Carriers, Street Vendors, Counter Sales, and Other Paid Distribution Outside USPS®	0	0
	(4) Paid Distribution by Other Classes of Mail Through the USPS (e.g. First-Class Mail®)	0	0
c. Total Paid Distribution (Sum of 15b (1), (2),(3), and (4))		222	215
d. Free or Nominal Rate Distribution (By Mail and Outside the Mail)	(1) Free or Nominal Rate Outside-County Copies Included on PS Form 3541	61	61
	(2) Free or Nominal Rate In-County Copies Included on PS Form 3541	0	0
	(3) Free or Nominal Rate Copies Mailed at Other Classes Through the USPS (e.g. First-Class Mail)	0	0
	(4) Free or Nominal Rate Distribution Outside the Mail (Carriers or other means)	0	0
e. Total Free or Nominal Rate Distribution (Sum of 15d (1), (2), (3) and (4))		61	61
f. Total Distribution (Sum of 15c and 15e)		283	276
g. Copies not Distributed (See Instructions to Publishers #4 (page #3))		540	523
h. Total (Sum of 15f and g)		823	799
i. Percent Paid (15c divided by 15f times 100)		78%	78%

16. Publication of Statement of Ownership
☐ If the publication is a general publication, publication of this statement is required. Will be printed in the WINTER 2007 issue of this publication.
☐ Publication not required

17. Signature and Title of Editor, Publisher, Business Manager, or Owner

Susan E. Lewis, VP & Publisher, Periodicals

Date: 10/1/2007

I certify that all information furnished on this form is true and complete. I understand that anyone who furnishes false or misleading information on this form or who omits material or information requested on the form may be subject to criminal sanctions (including fines and imprisonment) and/or civil sanctions (including civil penalties).